T5-BCL-347

EDITED BY

DAVID J. RANDOLPH

WITH SPECIAL ASSISTANCE FROM BILL GARRETT

VENTURES IN SONG

EDITED BY

DAVID J. RANDOLPH

for the
COMMISSION on WORSHIP of THE UNITED
METHODIST CHURCH

WITH SPECIAL ASSISTANCE FROM BILL GARRETT

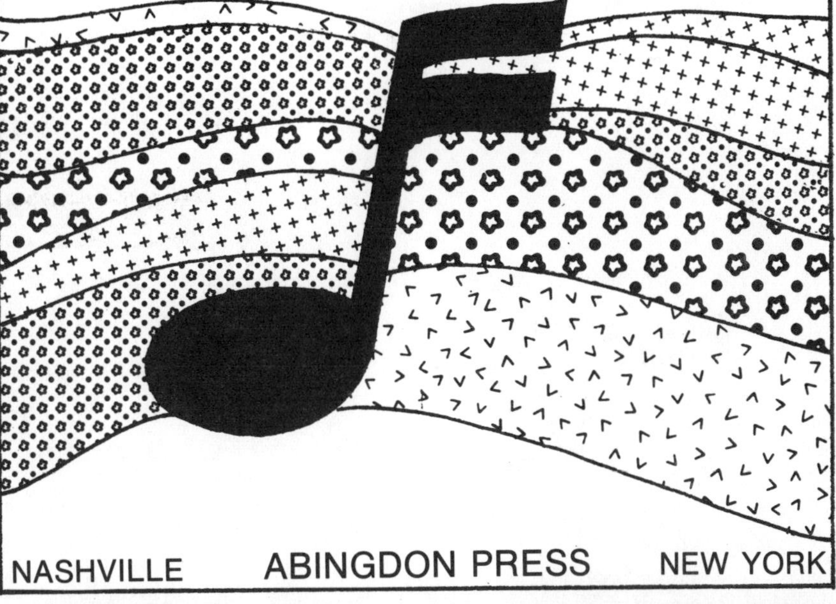

NASHVILLE ABINGDON PRESS NEW YORK

Ventures in Song

ISBN 0-687-43682-6

MANUFACTURED BY THE
PARTHENON PRESS AT NASHVILLE,
TENNESSEE, UNITED STATES OF AMERICA

CONTENTS

Ventures in Song is a collection of songs for a pilgrimage. The collection is a contribution to a global search—a search for new meaning and a search for more adequate ways to express meaning. The collection is not comprehensive. It is not the result of a contest. It is a sampling.

In *Ventures in Song* you will find
*** traditional spirituals,
coming alive in today's struggles
*** old hymns,
filled with new meaning
*** new music in folk, rock, jazz, and twist,
shedding light on our common experiences
*** a traditional hymn in a new idiom, and
*** a traditional hymn tune with new words,
encouraging us to try new ways
*** original songs never before published,
refreshing our spirits with the sound of now
*** songs of anguish,
communicating fear, frustration and pain
*** songs of joy,
celebrating the real
*** the words of prophets, old and new,
piercing our apathy and hypocrisy
*** songs that are questions, and
*** songs that are answers,
always probing, risking, venturing

Guitar pickers and strummers will rejoice with all the guitar chordings. Novice guitar players will find help in the guitar chord chart. Pianists and organists will have fun with the accompaniments that have been provided with many of the songs. Choir directors who like a lot of unison singing, or choir directors who are blessed with singers who are good at improvising harmonies, will appreciate the fact that melody lines are included for all except one of the songs. We just couldn't secure the permission to use more than the words to a few of the stanzas of that one song. Sorry about that.

Where will *Ventures in Song* be used? Well, you name it! We're prepared for a lot of surprises. This volume may turn up in:
*** pew racks for use in formal Sunday worship services
*** loose-leaf binders for use in informal celebrations
*** meeting rooms of fellowship groups of youth, students, or adults
*** mod-wrapped boxes under Christmas trees with teen-agers' names affixed
*** stacks on resource tables at conferences and conventions
*** the hands of retreat-goers
*** the secluded stacks of some library in a little town in Vermont
*** the living room of your home, always lying open on your piano
*** your bedroom, right next to your guitar or autoharp
*** the bandshell of your local park
*** the hospital room of a friend

As we said, you name it!

Ventures in Song can be used as:
*** a hymnal or songbook in its own right
*** a supplement to the hymnal that now stands in your pew racks
*** the beginnings of an expandable, loose-leaf collection for your choir
*** a supplement or complement to *Ventures in Worship* and *Ventures in Worship 2* (and any other volumes that may be published in this series)
*** a doodle book for bored worshipers

We sincerely hope that *Ventures in Song* will be seen as only a beginning. May the *Ventures in Song* flow like a cascading stream. If you are writing new music, or if you know of someone who is, send samples (wherever possible, please include words, music, guitar chording, and piano accompaniment) to:

The Project on Worship
1908 Grand Avenue
Nashville, Tennessee 37203

And when you send samples, please send along a statement for permission to use the music.

Thanks

The major purposes of this volume are: (1) to share selected materials gathered in the Project on Worship, (2) to supplement available materials for worship, and (3) to stimulate further exploration for faithful and vital music for the worship of the church.

If these purposes are achieved it will be because of the work of many people. Special thanks go to Bishop Lance Webb, Chairman of the General Commission on Worship of The United Methodist Church. His colleagues on the Commission have helped, especially the Rev. Dr. William F. Dunkle, Jr., Vice-Chairman; and the Rev. Hoyt Hickman, Executive Secretary.

The Project on Worship, out of which this work grows, is a joint venture of the Commission on Worship and the Board of Evangelism of The United Methodist Church. Special thanks go to Bishop Noah W. Moore, Jr., Chairman of the Board, and to Joseph H. Yeakel, General Secretary. Without their interest and support, this Project would not have been possible.

The Rev. Eugene Holmes is Chairman of the Committee on Resources for Worship which has included Mrs. Wilbur Longstreth, Paul M. Davis, Robert Hoffelt, and the Rev. Joe Harding while this work was being prepared. Their suggestions and judgments have been invaluable.

William F. Burns, Phillip Dietterich, Cecil Lapo and others have given valuable guidance, especially on the musical side.

Much correspondence and related work has been necessary. To Mrs. Mary Barbour and to Miss Hilda Young go thanks for service both effective and sensitive.

To the musicians and their business associates goes a loud cheer of thanks. They, of course, have supplied the artistry without which—nothing. It was a bright day when Dorothy Gros wrote back from Hawthorn Books, "Permission granted. Please make proper acknowledgments. Good luck!" Everything was beautiful when John Ragsdale told us he was "most happy" to grant permission for Ray Stevens' number. And Ewald Bash, of the American Lutheran Church, responded to a letter which listed the Christian Community Section Staff, writing, "I like a letterhead that says Glenn Evans—Appalachia. If you want, give a minimum fee to Appalachia." It is that spirit, which we have encountered again and again when we needed it, which has made this venture a joy.

Not everything is here, of course. *The Hymnal for Young Christians,* published by F.E.L.; *Hymns for Now* from the Walther League; and *New Wine,* from the Southern California-Arizona Conference of The United Methodist Church will be around for a long time, we hope. Publication data on them, and other sources

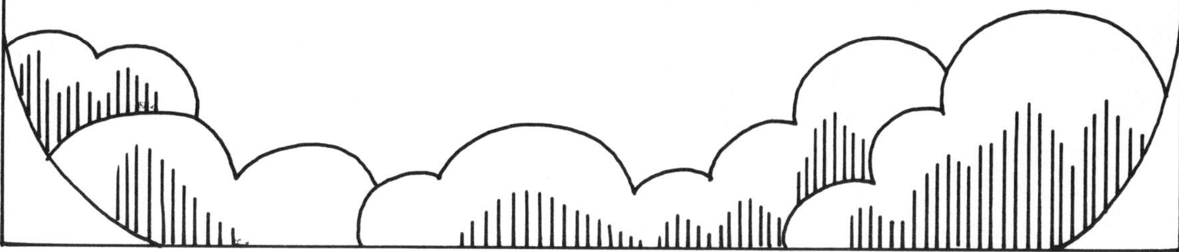

of songs and hymns, may be found in *Ventures in Worship* and *Ventures in Worship 2,* edited by David James Randolph and published by Abingdon Press in 1969 and 1970 respectively.

To David James Randolph and William H. Garrett has come the responsibility for the preparation of this volume. Together, they have proposed the selections. Mr. Randolph carried the basic administration of the project and wrote the introduction. Mr. Garrett supervised the musical arrangements and wrote the interludes. In the end, it was more than just two people working side by side, and for the new thing that emerged, Editors Randolph and Garrett offer thanks to God.

More than most projects, this has involved the families of the editors. As always, Juanita encouraged Dave; and Marianne, Bill. But especially, they were thinking about their children and their future as they worked, and the children helped. To David, III, and Tracey Randolph, and to Susan, Scott, and Michelle Garrett go very special thanks.

David James Randolph
William H. Garrett
Nashville, Tennessee

A Word About What's Going on Here

A new song
a new song
yes
a new song is being sung.

On the streets
on beaches
on campuses
yes
in churches
a new song is being sung.

A new song
of praise
of people
of peace

And thus
an old song
an old song
is being sung.

Long hairs sing it
and yes
gray hairs sing it
and
even people with no hairs
sing it.
Across the gaps
we are learning to sing
to one another.

Across the gaps
of years
of color
of sex
of place
of nation

Wearelearningtosingagain.

Where did it come from?
Well, there are those
who say that God whistled
right after He turned on the lights. Wow!
Jesus picked up the tune
and danced and died and danced to it.
And the Spirit is humming now. Hear Her?

These now songs are like that.
Some old songs suddenly new
(like Arlo Guthrie of the Woodstock
Generation singing "Amazing Grace"
which surprises Grandma not at all).
Some new songs suddenly old
(seems like we've been singing "They'll Know
We Are Christians by Our Love"
all our lives).
Some never before published
(Hurray! They're harder to find
than you think. Got some?
Send them in. This is a
beginning not an ending.)
Some written for use in church,
Some written for use on stereos,
Some written for no use at all,
just for the fun of it.

Will it last,
will it last? Some ask.

Some of it will.
Yes, some of it will probably
be sung centuries from now.
Not just popularity of a week
(would Jesus have made the Top-40
with Sermon on the mount?)
But the ability to say something that
lingers.

There is here music that will linger
linger yes
stay in your mind
twist at your heart
in nighttime hours.

Some may be only
music of the moment.
Don't worry about that
tear it out and
give it to the paper drive
save a tree.

The mission—that is what counts.
The mission.
Not getting "with it"
but getting with Him—
in the midst of life.

The mission is movement
from praise
through confession
through proclamation
to commitment
which means grappling
with peace
and love and justice
(there is no love without justice)
freedom
ecology
food
community,
spiraling upward through
Celebration.
God and man
faith and culture,
church and world,
distinct but interpenetrating,
interacting
swinging

Beginning and ending
in praise of God.

The mission—that's what's going on here.

We have been trying to write theology
in a new style
And discovered that
The new style of theology cannot be written.
You have to sing and dance and live it.

Sing and dance, then,
Praise God and seek peace,
Confess sin and feed the hungry,
Proclaim good news to the poor
Give yourself to the community beyond
communities and
Celebrate.

D. J. R.

It's Time for Praise

Come on, now! It's time for praise!
Lift your voice hum the tune . . .
For the Lord has risen, it is true!
So clap your hands to Ray Repp's tune
Twist to Werle's Joyful, Joyful
Praise the Lord in your very own way
Hurray! Hurray! It's Easter day
If we had ten thousand tongues
What a song we'd sing

If the Spirit of the Lord is upon us
How can we remain silent?
Let's not wait for the rocks to shout
Let's turn up the volume
Let it all hang out

And don't stop with the music that's here
Make your own

Sing "He's Got the Whole World in His Hands"
Think about the wonder of creation
Write some words that say what you feel
Now, say out loud the words you wrote
s a y t h e m s l o w l y

SAYTHEMFASTANDLOUD

Say them again—feel (da da) the beat (da dee da)
Whistle a tune that fits the rhythm of your words
Grab three friends
Say, "Hey, listen to this"
Sing your song Let them help

Come on, now! It's time for praise!

W. H. G.

The truth may be a dream far away
It may be close at hand
But the truth that's inside a man
Has such a hard time getting out.

All have sinned and fallen short
But you'd never know it
If all you ever saw were the false fronts.

We're lonely like the desperate man
Frustrated—from having tried so hard, in vain
Sure that God is dead.

Don't just sit there and pretend that you're alive
When you're really dead
You may miss the glory of the morning.

Focus on the never-dying love of one who died
To break the chains of death
And let your soul cry out for release
And let your ears hear others crying
And let your eyes see others dying.

Then, let your desperation slowly turn
To search . . .

W. H. G.

Ballad of a Desperate Man

Hank Sable

Stanza 1
When there was no voice to believe in
My dreams were driftin' far away
When my love decided she was leaving
Could not find a reason for to stay.

CHORUS
Oh I was a desperate man
And all my thought of freedom ceased
Till I found your lovin' hand
My soul cried out to be released.

Stanza 2
I was left alone to seek another sky
With a love inside I longed to share,
Empty rooms that could not tell me why
Open doors with no one there.

CHORUS

Stanza 3
I think about the time I spent alone
Searching in the dark of night.
I think I finally found a home,
I think I finally seen the light.

CHORUS

Stanza 4
In your eyes I found my dream again,
Gentle words that set my feeling free.
I need your love by me, my friend
For it's you that holds that certain key.

CHORUS

SAY IT, BROTHER

What have your eyes seen?
Is there not much to elicit hope?
What have your ears heard?

Spread the news!
Wherever life breaks out afresh
Like a bud on a rosebush
Wherever love captures a human spirit
Who has known only jealousy and hate
Wherever honesty takes over
Like a breath of fresh air

If you believe that God is
Don't keep the goodies to yourself
If you have been resurrected from death
to life
Put it into words; write a poem; hum what
it feels like
To be free—let it be!
If there's a word that needs to be said
Wrap it around a complete thought
Emphasize its beat
And dance all around its meaning
Dance, until the word becomes flesh
And maybe, just maybe, the music of the
word
Will hit home—somewhere, somehow, in
someone.

Say it, brother!

W. H. G.

BUT DON'T STOP WITH WORDS

And the Lord said, "Whom shall I send?"

Well, let's not have dead silence.
The Lord of the dance is making beautiful music
And he wants to make of your whole life a symphony.

If, in the honesty and integrity of your confession,
And, in the light of your affirmations,
And, in the thrill of the praises that you chanted,
There is any life—
if any love
if any hope
if any incentive
Then, let it show.

If it is life you say you choose
Then, look alive
act alive
make of your life a symphony
a rock opera
a turn-on musical

Act in such a reconciling way that peace
Is colored a bright green all around you.

Stand in an ocean of love,
Guided by the rudder of justice
And full of song
Don't just say love
Don't just think justice
Sing love—overflow with caring
Fill your institutions with justice

Shout with great joy when you are free
Rattle your cage—with great noise—when you are a slave
And when your brother and sister are not free

Sing about the air your breathe
Sing yourself into action when the air isn't fit to breathe

Write songs, poems—make news—when your brother is starving

And through it all
Let's remember
They'll know we are Christians by our love.

But then, maybe all you want to be is a noisy gong!

W. H. G.

the times they are a-changin'

Bob Dylan

Stanza 1 "Come gather 'round people wherever you roam
And admit that the waters around you have grown
And accept it that soon you'll be drenched to the bone,
If your time to you is worth savin'
Then you better start swimmin' or you'll sink like a stone,
For THE TIMES THEY ARE A-CHANGIN'

Stanza 4 Come mothers and fathers,
Throughout the land
And don't criticize
What you can't understand.
Your sons and your daughters
Are beyond your command
Your old road is
Rapidly agin'
Please get out of the new one
If you can't lend your hand
For THE TIMES THEY ARE A-CHANGIN'

Stanza 5 The line it is drawn
The curse it is cast
The slow one now will
Later be fast.
As the present now
Will later be past
The order is rapidly fadin'
And the first one now
Will later be last
For THE TIMES THEY ARE A-CHANGIN' "

PRAISE

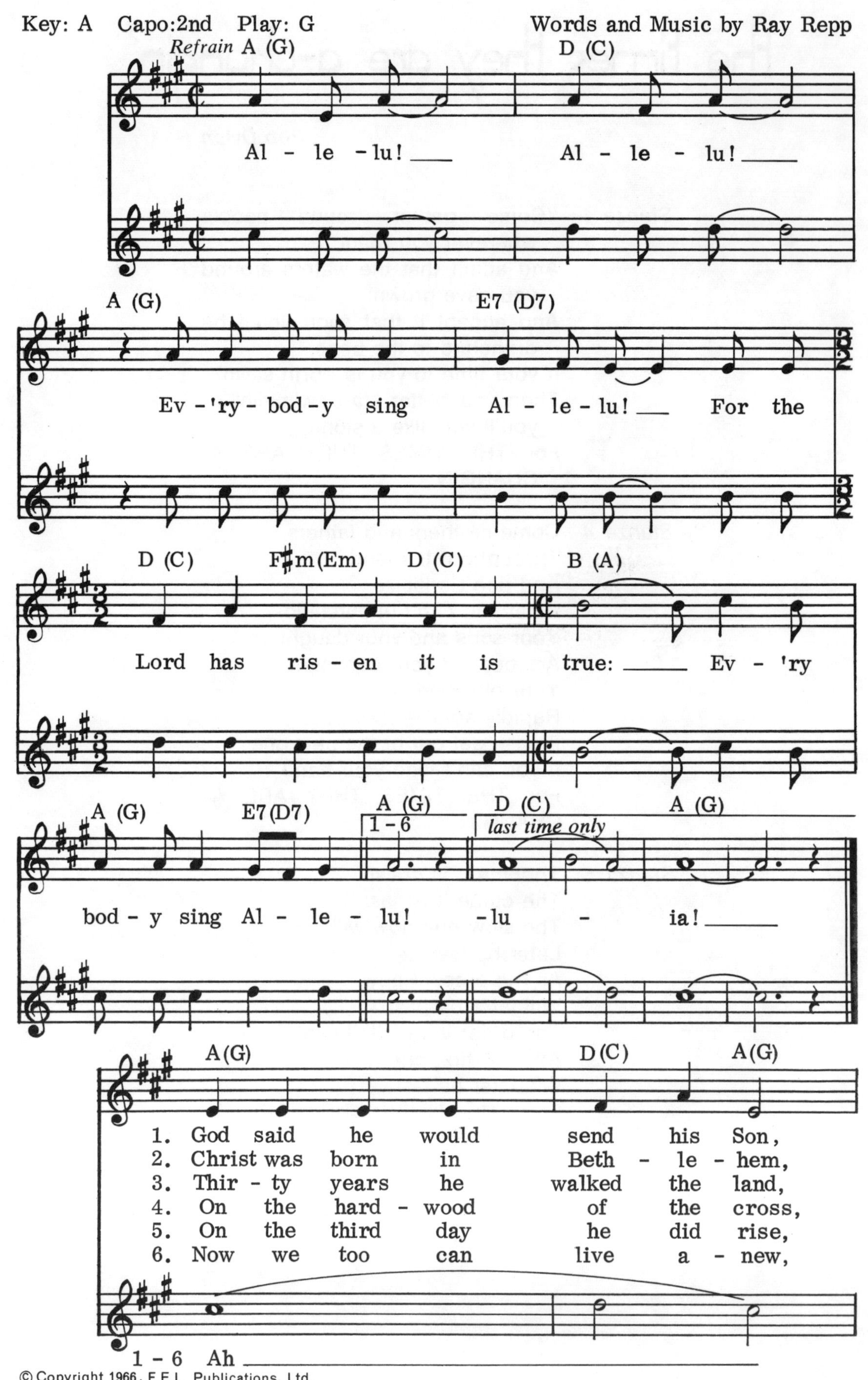
Allelu!
Key: A Capo:2nd Play: G
Words and Music by Ray Repp
Refrain A (G)
D (C)
Al - le - lu! Al - le - lu!
A (G)
E7 (D7)
Ev - 'ry - bod - y sing Al - le - lu! For the
D (C) F♯m(Em) D (C) B (A)
Lord has ris - en it is true: Ev - 'ry
A (G) E7(D7) A (G) D (C) A (G)
1 - 6
last time only
bod - y sing Al - le - lu! - lu - ia!
A(G) D(C) A(G)
1. God said he would send his Son,
2. Christ was born in Beth - le - hem,
3. Thir - ty years he walked the land,
4. On the hard - wood of the cross,
5. On the third day he did rise,
6. Now we too can live a - new,
1 - 6 Ah
© Copyright 1966, F.E.L. Publications, Ltd.
Los Angeles, Calif. Used with permission.

E7(D7) D(C) F♯m(Em) D(C)
Al - le - lu, Al - le - lu! ___ And sal - va - tion would be
Al - le - lu, Al - le - lu! ___ So that man would live a -
Al - le - lu, Al - le - lu! ___ To all in need he lent his
Al - le - lu, Al - le - lu! ___ He suf-fered and he died for
Al - le - lu, Al - le - lu! ___ Now he lives no more to
Al - le - lu, Al - le - lu! ___ Live in him need all we
Al - le - lu, Al - le - lu! ___ Ah ___
B(A) D(C) E7(D7)
won, Al - le - lu - ia!
gain, Al - le - lu - ia!
hand, Al - le - lu - ia!
us, Al - le - lu - ia!
die, Al - le - lu - ia!
do, Al - le - lu - ia!
Ah ___ Al - le - lu - ia! ___
Clap Your Hands
Words and music by Ray Repp
Refrain
C F C F C
All you peo - ples, clap your hands (x) (x) and shout for
G7 Em Am C F
joy: The Lord has made all man - kind one, ___

C G7 C Fine
So raise your voi - ces high!
Verses
C F C
1. All cre- a - tion shows the glo - ry of the
2. The strength of God is great; he rules from sea to
3. The King of all the earth has made his mes - sage
4. The king - dom of the Lord was made for all the
5. Let ev - 'ry man a - live re - mem - ber your com -
G7 F C F C
Lord; The earth pro - claims his hand - i - work; the
sea, And all cre - a - tion knows the might and
known, That we should of - fer him our - selves and
good, Those who want to live in peace
mand, That ev - 'ry day in ev - 'ry way we
F C G7 C
sky cries out his word. Night and day sing
glo - ry of his deeds. So ev - 'ry queen and
ev - 'ry - thing we own. We do this by the
and broth - er - hood. So with your fel - low
love our fel - low man. If this com - mand is
F C Am
out the glo - ries all a - bout, So
king, join in now as we sing, And
way we live through ev - 'ry day, So
man let's all join hand to hand, And
done, the vic - t'ry will be won, And
F G7 C G7
praise the Lord with shouts of joy.
praise the Lord with shouts of joy.
live each day in peace and joy.
praise the Lord with shouts of joy.
we'll all live in peace and joy.

He's Got the Whole World in His Hands

Alleluia

A setting of Psalm 148
by Joe Pfister
C, Capo 2
Chorus
C F C
Al - le - lu - ia, Al - le - lu - ia,
Em F G F C
Al - le - lu - ia, Praise ye the Lord!
repeat chorus several times at beginning and at end of hymn ad libitum
1. You high-est heav-ens,_ You an-gel hosts, Lift up your voic-es,_ Sing to the Lord!
2. You fire and hail,_ You snow and frost, You storm-y winds,_ Sing to the Lord!
3. You deep sea mon-sters,_ You fly-ing birds, Lift up your voic-es,_ Sing to the Lord!
4. You kings and prin-ces,_ You men of state, Let all the na-tions_ Sing to the Lord!
F C F C D G
F C F C F C
You sun and moon,_ You shin-ing stars, Lift up your voic-es,_ sing to the Lord!
Moun-tains and hills,_ Fruit trees and cedars, Let all that grows_ sing to the Lord!
You beasts and cat-tle,_ You creep-ing things, Lift up your voic-es,_ sing to the Lord!
Young men and mai-dens,_ Old men and children, Let all cre - a-tion_ sing to the Lord!
G G7 C F C
last chorus
Al - le - lu - ia, Al - le - lu - ia,
Em F E G C
Al - le - lu - ia, Praise ye the Lord!_

Joyful, Joyful, We Adore Thee

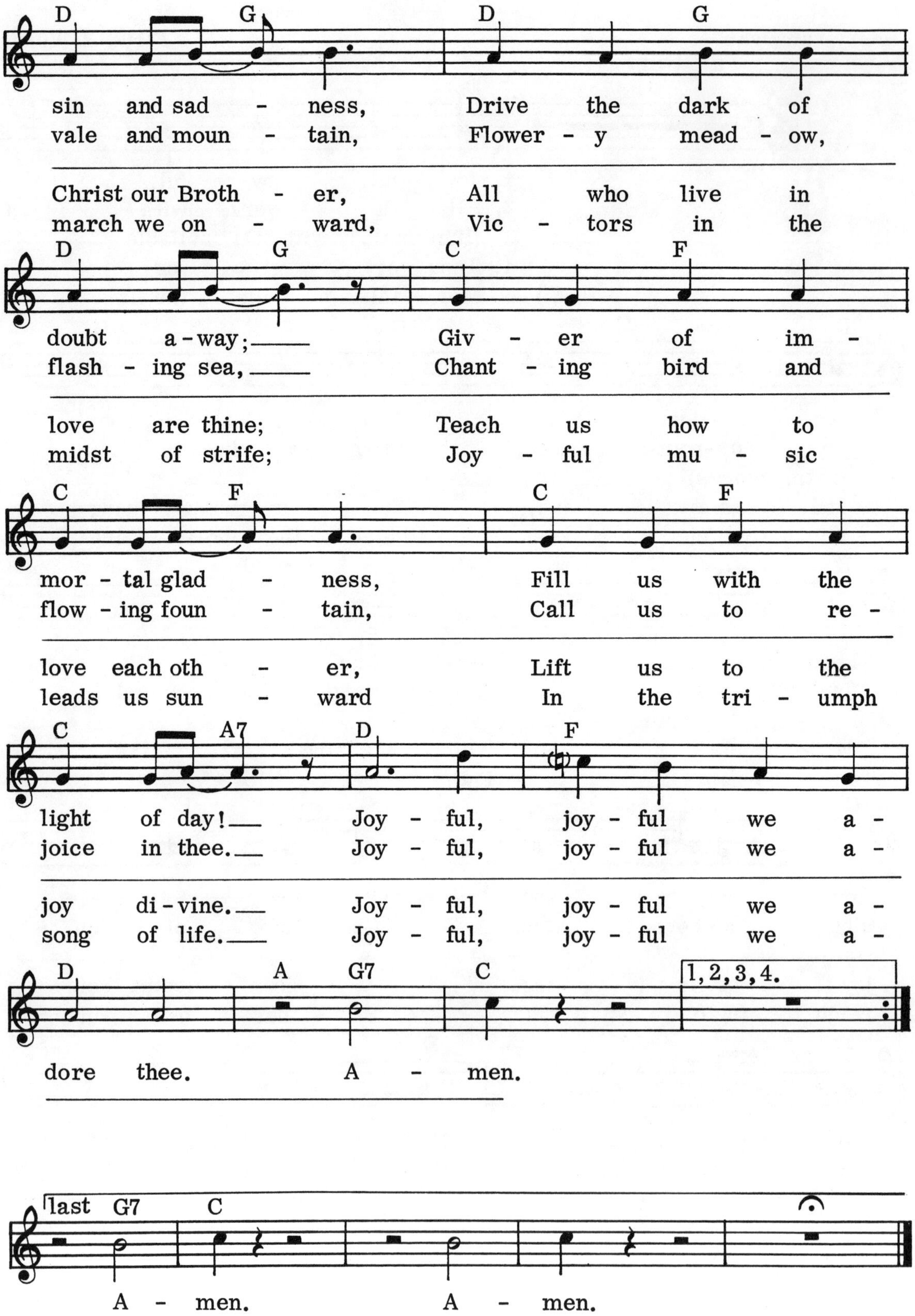
D G D G
sin and sad - ness, Drive the dark of
vale and moun - tain, Flower - y mead - ow,
Christ our Broth - er, All who live in
march we on - ward, Vic - tors in the
D G C F
doubt a - way; Giv - er of im -
flash - ing sea, Chant - ing bird and
love are thine; Teach us how to
midst of strife; Joy - ful mu - sic
C F C F
mor - tal glad - ness, Fill us with the
flow - ing foun - tain, Call us to re -
love each oth - er, Lift us to the
leads us sun - ward In the tri - umph
C A7 D F
light of day! Joy - ful, joy - ful we a -
joice in thee. Joy - ful, joy - ful we a -
joy di - vine. Joy - ful, joy - ful we a -
song of life. Joy - ful, joy - ful we a -
D A G7 C 1, 2, 3, 4.
dore thee. A - men.
last G7 C
A - men. A - men.

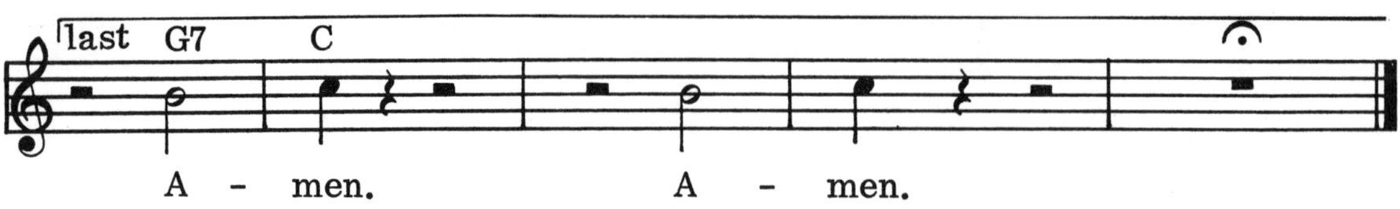

O For a Thousand Tongues to Sing

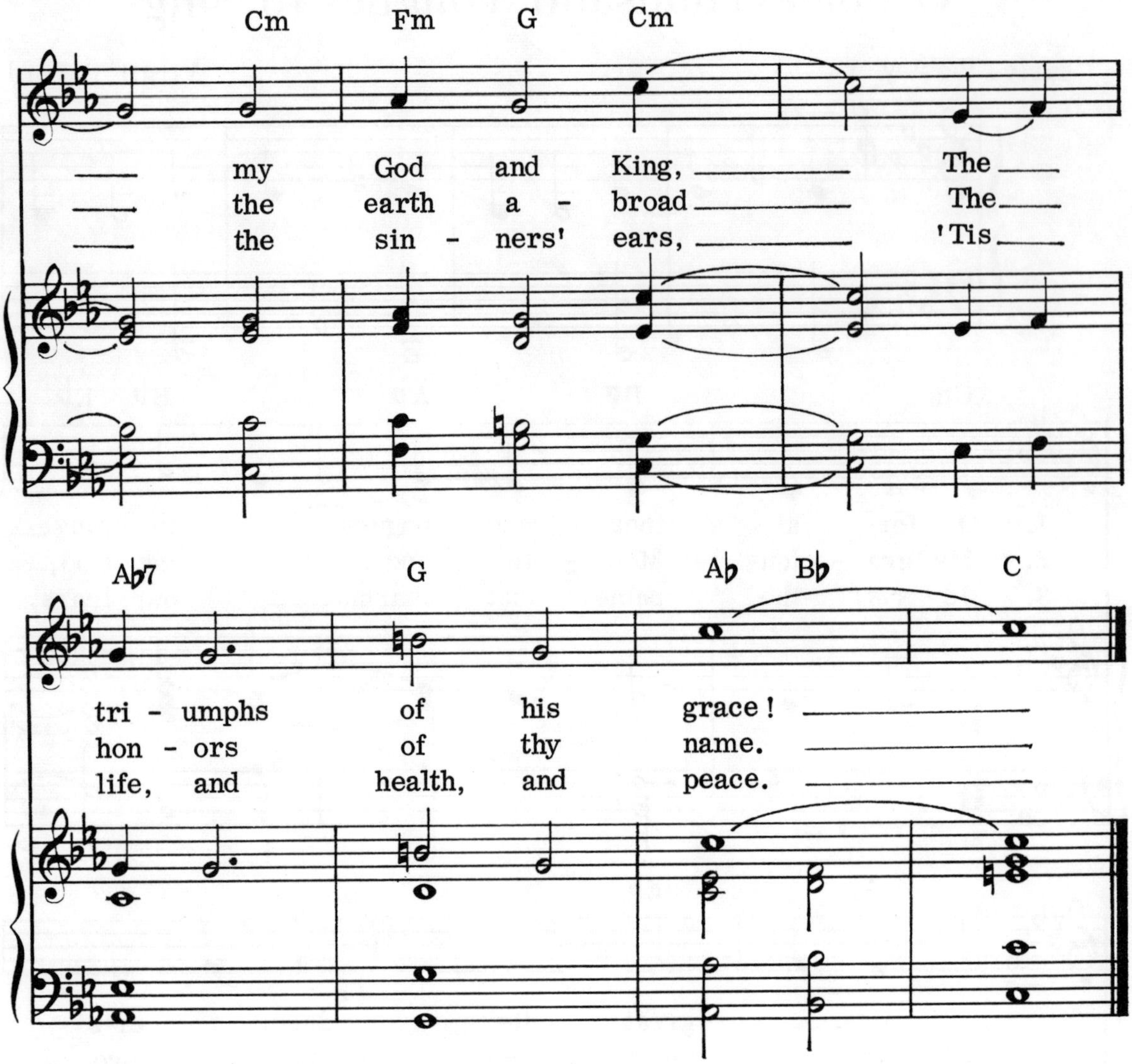

Cm Fm G Cm
my God and King, The
the earth a - broad The
the sin - ners' ears, 'Tis
Ab7 G Ab Bb C
tri - umphs of his grace!
hon - ors of thy name.
life, and health, and peace.

The Spirit of the Lord Is upon Us

Phil West

Chorus
Am Em
The Spir - it of the Lord is up - on us!
Am Em
This is a hap - py day,
1. Be -
2. Be -
3. Be -
4. When

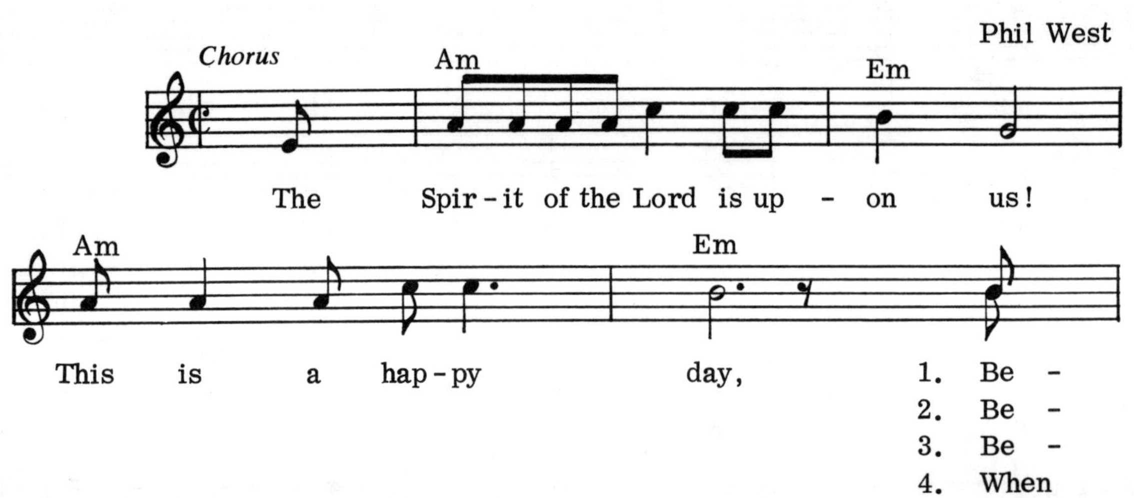

Am G
cause we pro - claim good news to the poor and
cause now the blind eyes o - pen to the dawn and
cause free -dom time is break - ing with the dawn and a
all fall ___ down in the peace of ___ God and
F G7 C
free - dom to those in chains.
e - ven the deaf must hear.
day to ___ sing with God.
love ___ comes home for us all.
1.E 2.C Verses C Am
The 1. With smoke on the riv - er
The 2. With board - ed ___ win - dows,
The 3. When bonds break ___ o - pen,
C Am C
call down the wind and fight - ing a - gainst the
cry in the dark and blood on the al - ley
run down the dawn, and all ___ the old walls
G7 C Am F G
wall, With chains on the roof - tops,
wall, With glass on the pave-ment, Pray for the day when
fall, With dark - ness_ fad - ing,
F G E
love comes home for us all! ___ The
(to chorus)
LOVE

Prayer of Confession

(Morning Song)

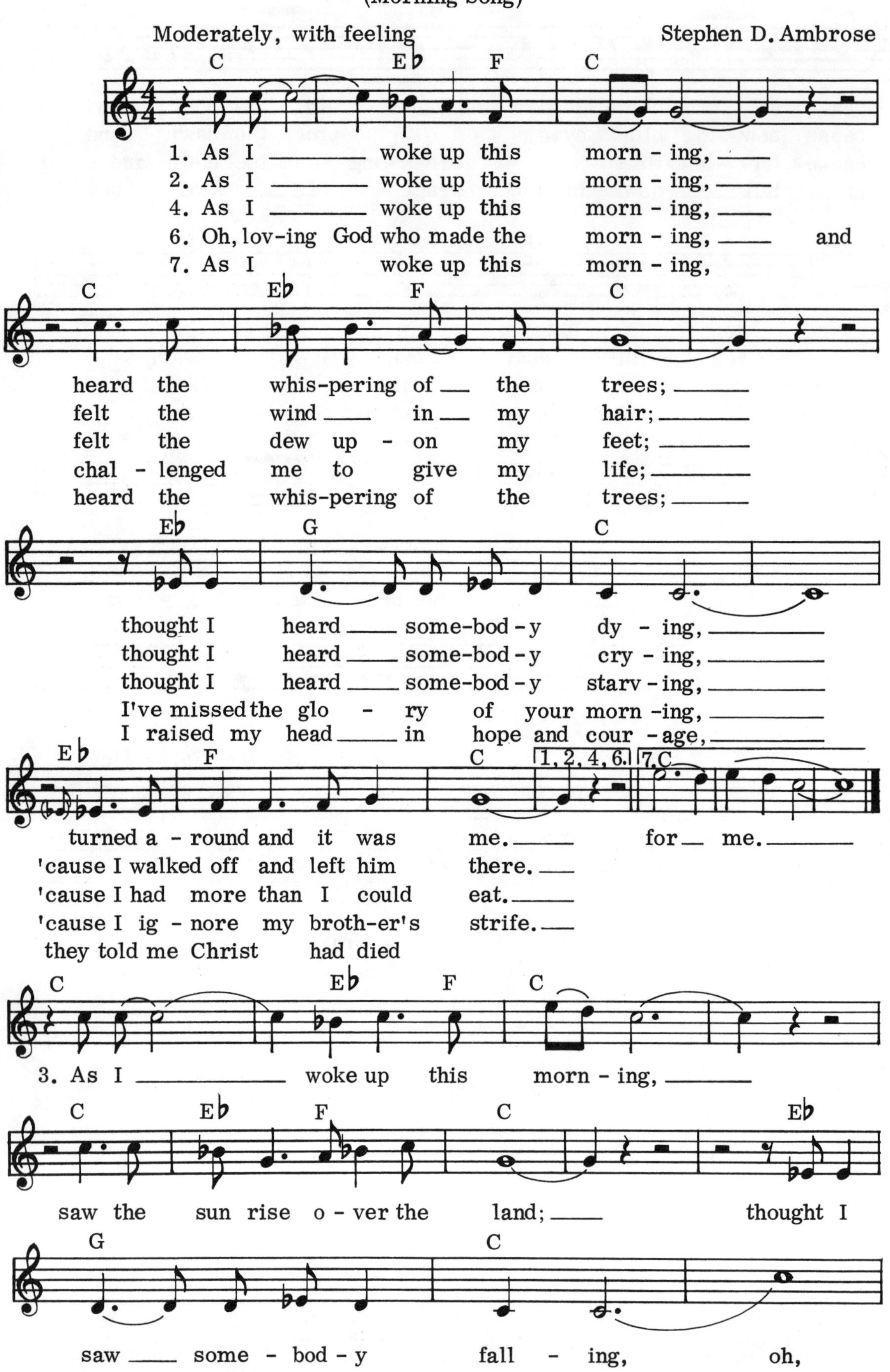

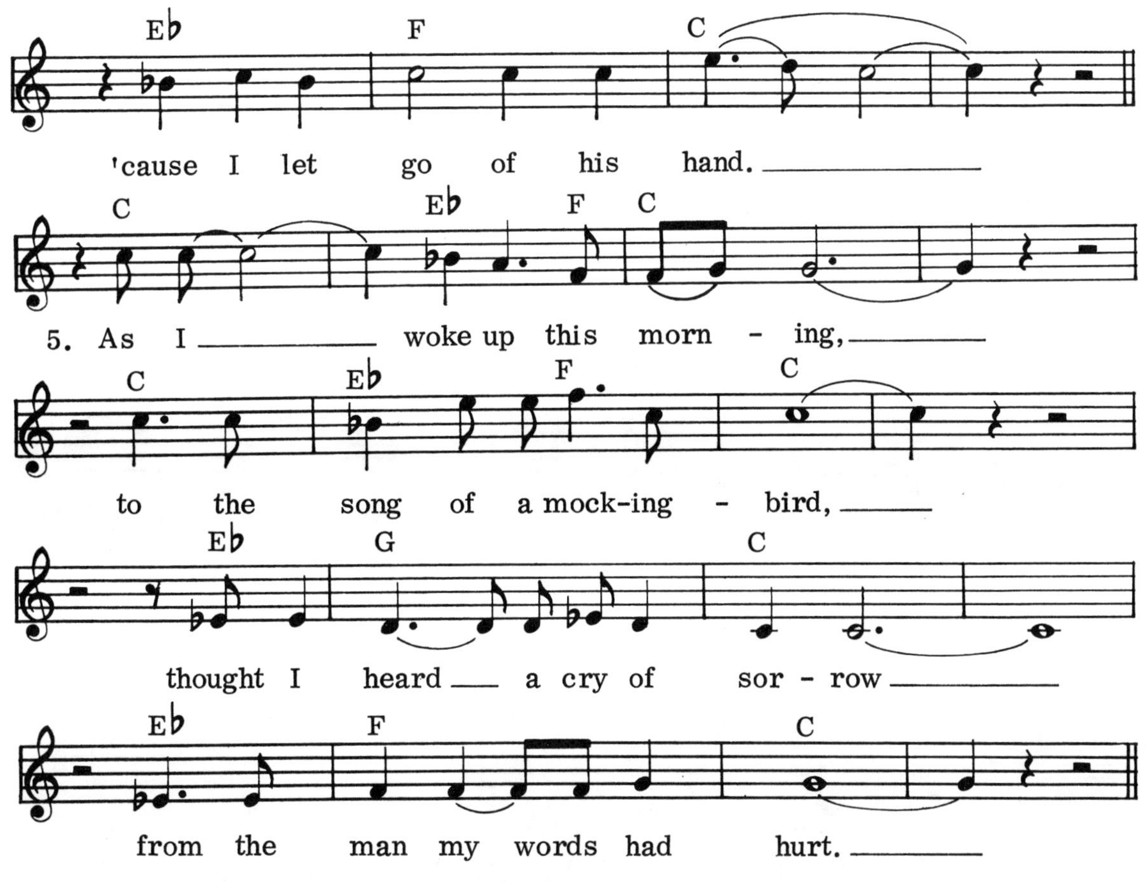

Lord's Prayer

West Indies

New Christ Cardiac Hero

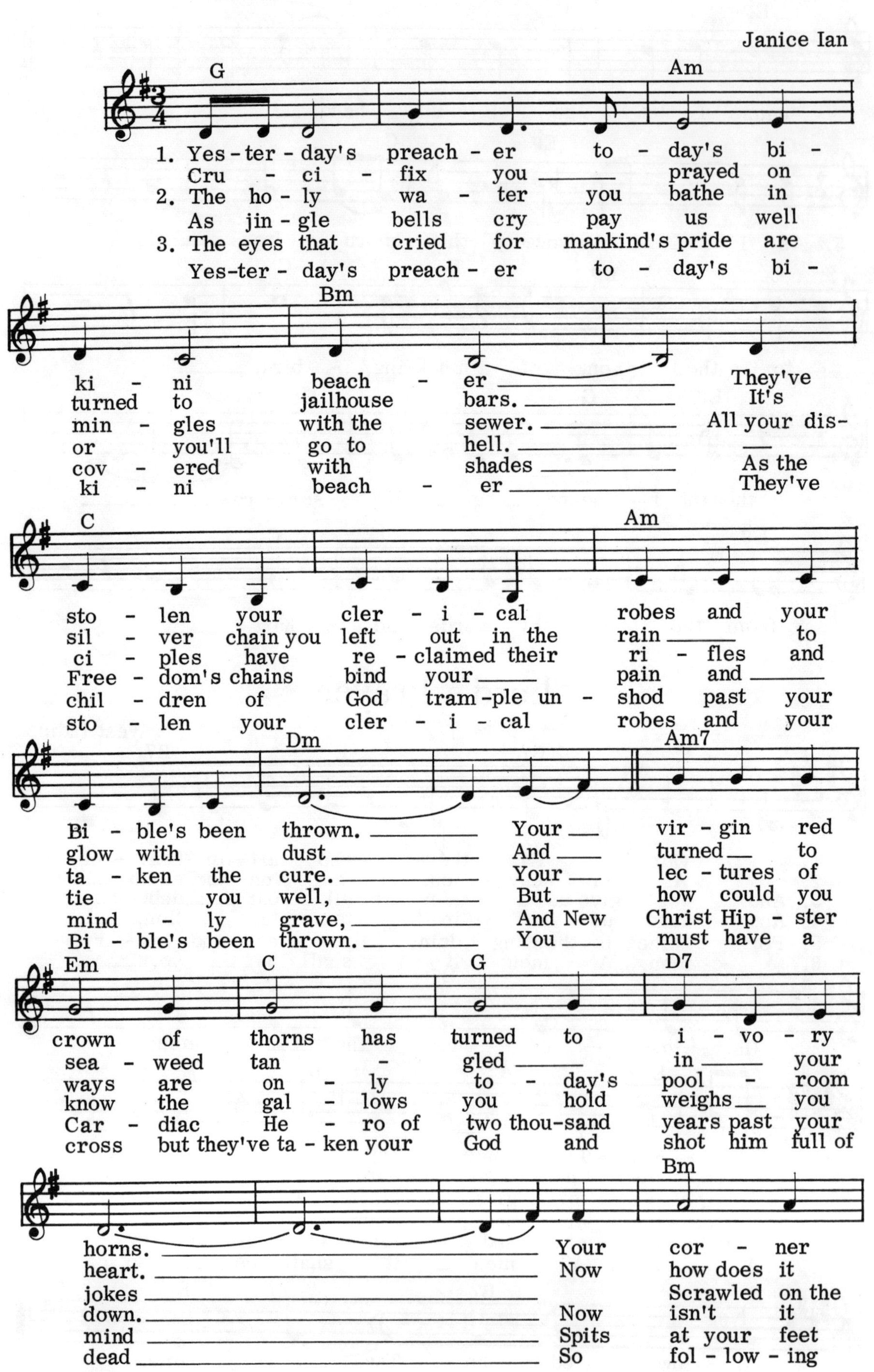

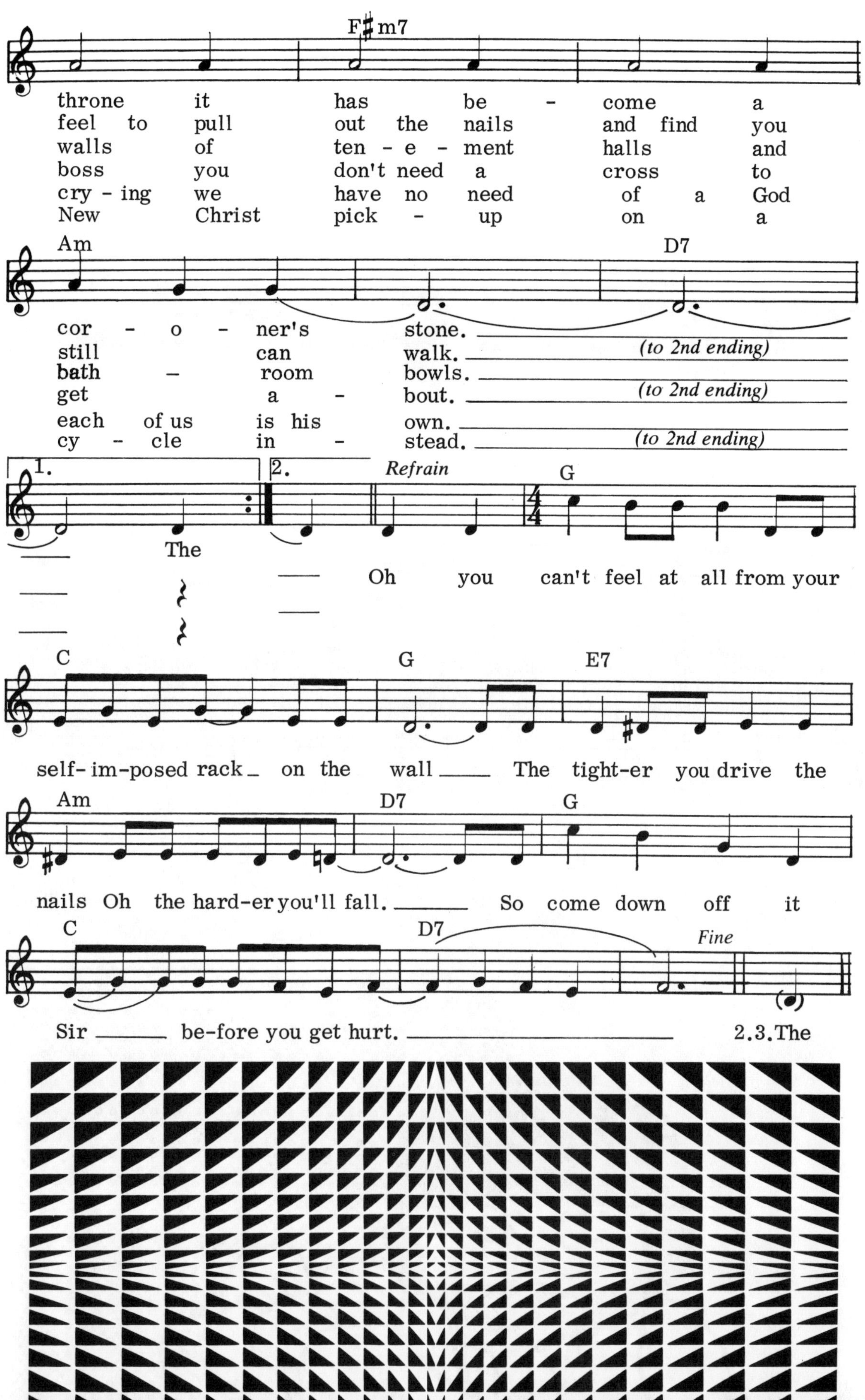
F♯m7
throne it has be - come a
feel to pull out the nails and find you
walls of ten - e - ment halls and
boss you don't need a cross to
cry - ing we have no need of a God
New Christ pick - up on a
Am
D7
cor - o - ner's stone.
still can walk.
(to 2nd ending)
bath - room bowls.
get a - bout.
(to 2nd ending)
each of us is his own.
cy - cle in - stead.
(to 2nd ending)
1.
2.
Refrain
G
The
Oh you can't feel at all from your
C
G
E7
self-im-posed rack on the wall The tight-er you drive the
Am
D7
G
nails Oh the hard-er you'll fall. So come down off it
C
D7
Fine
Sir be-fore you get hurt. 2.3.The

Judas

R. K. Hudnut — J. L. Bell

Chorus

C F C
Ju - das, oh, ——— Ju - das He

G F G C
knew that he was a - ble and he knew that he was right.

G F G Dm C Fm7 C *Fine*
Ju - das left the ta - ble and went out to ___ the night.

Verses

C F G C
1. Ju - das was a tough guy, He was a self - made man. You
2. Ju - das did his own thing, The oth - ers could do theirs. In
3. Ju - das need-ed no one, But Je - sus need - ed him. He
4. Ju - das was a lon - er, He on - ly had twelve friends. It
5. Ju - das loved his mon - ey, He was the treas - ur - er. With
6. Ju - das the a - pos - tate, Played out his cho - sen role. He

F G C F G7 D. C.
of - ten used to hear him cry, "What I will do I can."
his own sphere he was a king, He had no need of prayers.
did all that he'd ev - er done To serve his ev - ery whim.
worked up - on his char - ac - ter, He used them for his ends.
mon - ey he could then be free, To be the con - quer-or.
was the "mas - ter of his fate, The cap - tain of his soul".

Christ is Changing Everything

Go, Tell It on the Mountain

American Folk Hymn
Arr. by John W. Work

D7 G G
si - lent flocks by night, Be - hold through - out the
lo! a - bove the earth Rang out the an - gel
hum-ble Christ was born, And God sent us sal -
A7 D D7 D.C.
heav - ens There shone a ho - ly light.
cho - rus That hailed our Sav - ior's birth.
va - tion That bless - ed Christ - mas morn.
Capo 3
Gonna Sing, My Lord
With motion (♩ = 98)
Joe Wise
Am G Am C
1. Gon-na sing, my Lord, for all that I'm
2. Gon-na love, my Lord, for all that I'm
3. Gon-na laugh, my Lord, for all that I'm
4. Gon-na die, my Lord, for all that I'm
5. Gon-na live, my Lord, for all that I'm
6. Gon-na sing, my Lord, for all that I'm
Am Dm
worth; Gon - na sing, my Lord, for all that I'm
worth; Gon - na love, my Lord, for all that I'm
worth; Gon - na laugh, my Lord, for all that I'm
worth; Gon - na die, my Lord, for all that I'm
worth; Gon - na live, my Lord, for all that I'm
worth; Gon - na sing, my Lord, for all that I'm
Am G
worth, Lord, Lord. Gon - na sing, my
worth, Lord, Lord. Gon - na love, my
worth, Lord, Lord. Gon - na laugh, my
worth, Lord, Lord. Gon - na die, my
worth, Lord, Lord. Gon - na live, my
worth, Lord, Lord. Gon - na sing, my

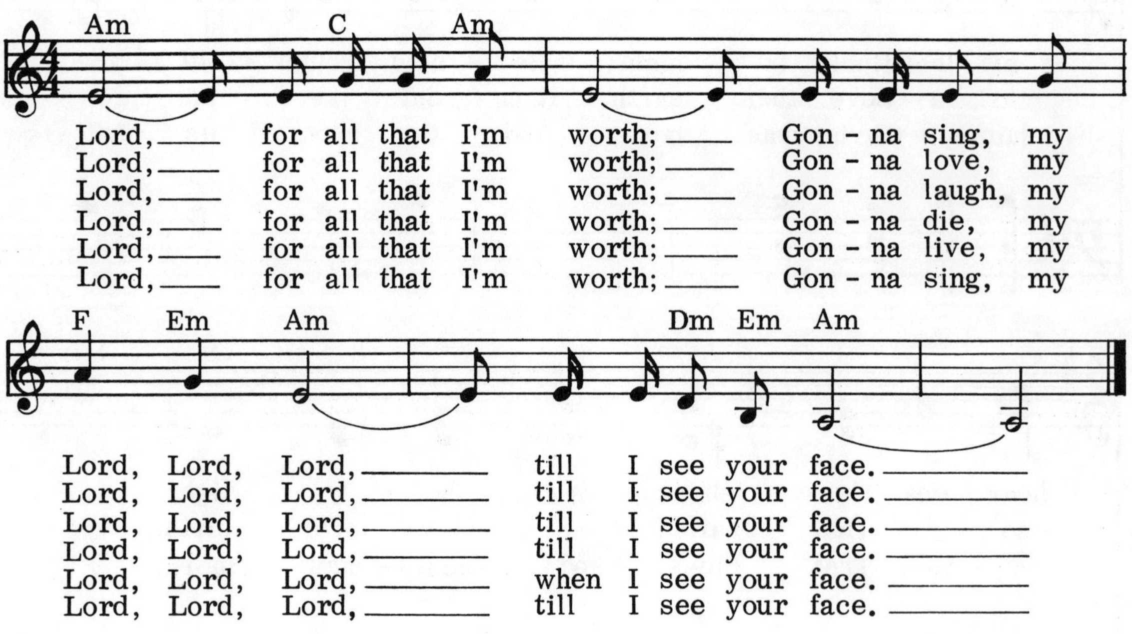

Hello, Goodbye

Ed Summerlin — Roger Ortmayer

Rock Beat

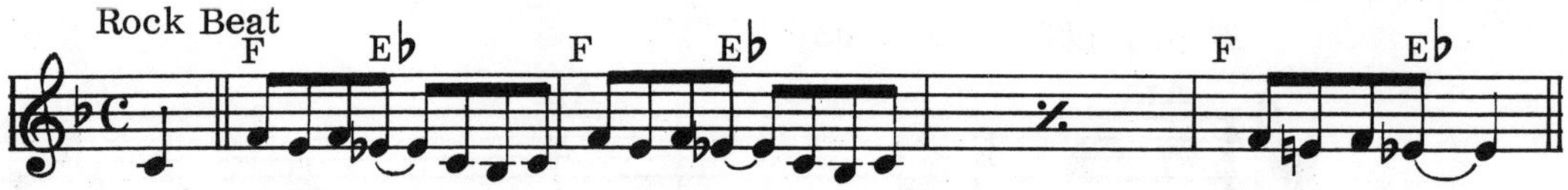

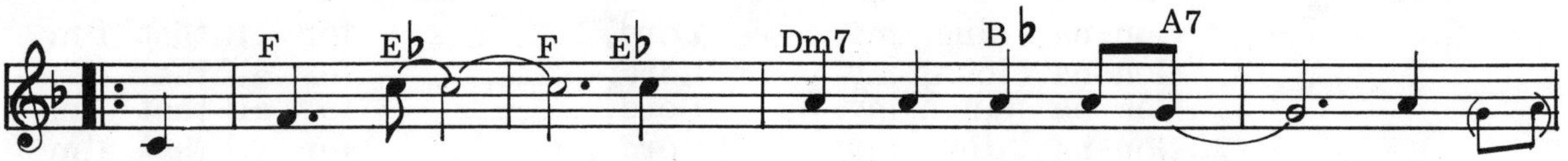

1. Hel - lo and did you hear the word And did you lis - ten well? Once you have heard the pre - cious word You have some - thing to tell. The
2. Good - bye and did you see the word In your midst for all to see? Be - fore you leave we must in - quire Of this gift so fine and free. The
3. Say man! and have you shared the word As strength and time al - low? Giv - en the word as bread to eat To all who hun - ger now? The

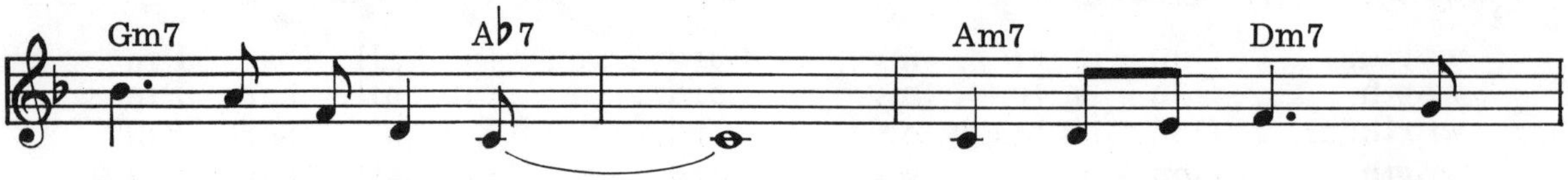

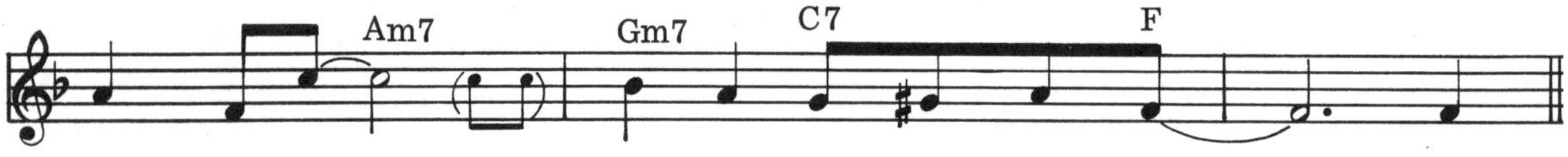

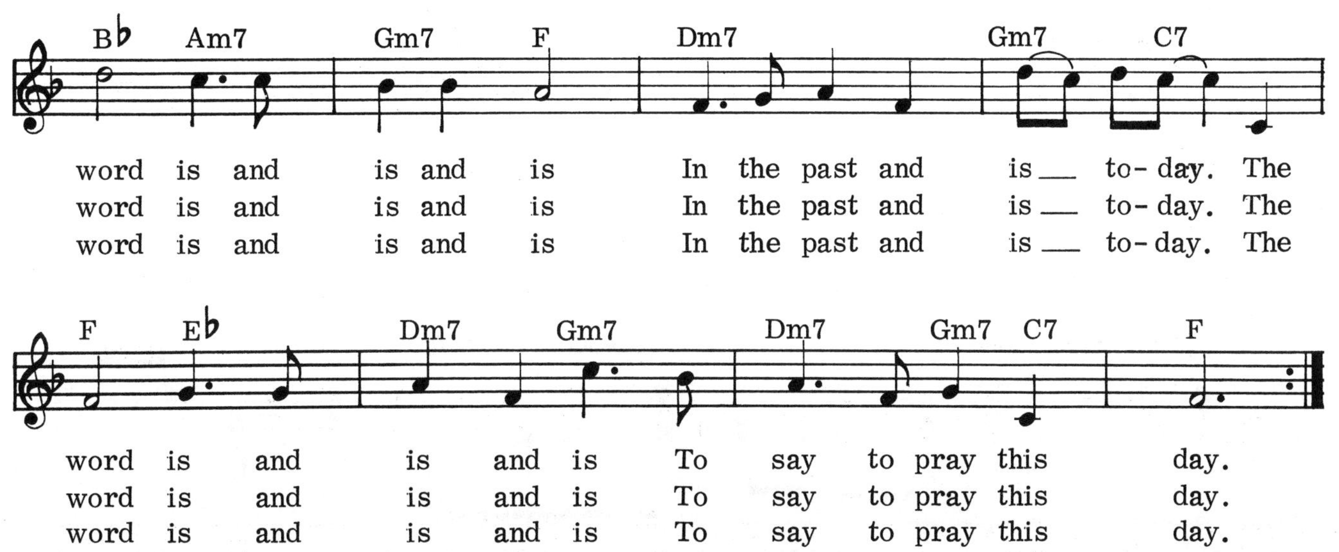

Let It Be

Words and Music by
John Lennon & Paul McCartney

Slow tempo (16 measures per minute)

C G Am F C G

F G7 C C G

1. When I find my-self ___ in times of trou - ble
2. ___ the bro - ken heart - ed peo - ple
3. *Instrumental* - - - - - - - - - - - - - - - - -
4. ___ the night ___ is cloud - y There is

Am G FM7 F6 C G
Moth-er Ma - ry comes to me Speak-ing words of wis - dom, let it
Liv-ing in ___ the world a-gree There will be an an - swer, let it
still a light _ that shines on me. Shine un - til to-mor - row, let it
F C Dm7 C G
be. ___ And in my hour of dark - ness She is
be. ___ For though they may be part - ed there is
be. ___ I wake up to the sound ___ of mu - sic
Am G FM7 F6 C G
stand-ing right in front _ of me ___ Speak-ing words of wis - dom, let it
still a chance that they will see ___ There will be an an - swer, let it
Moth-er Ma-ry comes _ to me Speak-ing words of wis - dom, let it

F C Dm7 C G Am G
be.
be.
- - - -
be.
Let it be, let it be, Let it be,
f
F C G
Whis-per words of wis - dom, let it be.
let it be, (v.2. Yeah) There will be an an - swer, let it be.
Whis-per words of wis - dom, let it be.
There will be an an - swer, let it be.
1, 3.
F C Dm7 C
2. And when
4. And when
2, 4.
F C Dm7 C G
Let it be,

Am
G
F
C
let it be, let it be, let it be,
G
F
C
Dm7
C
Whis-per words of wis-dom, let it be,
to Coda
F
Em
Dm7
C
B♭
F
G
F
C
F
C
Dm
C
f
G
F
C
D.S. al Coda
(Instrumental & Repeat)
CODA
G
F
G
C

Mine Eyes Have Seen the Glory

Julia Ward Howe

American Camp Meeting Tune

ter - ri - ble swift sword; His
dim and flar - ing lamps; His
ju - bi - lant, my feet! Our
die to make men free! While
soul of wrong his slave. Our
E♭ B♭ F B♭
truth is march - ing on.
day is march - ing on.
God is march - ing on.
God is march - ing on.
God is march - ing on.
Refrain
B♭
Glo - ry! glo - ry! Hal - le - lu - jah!
E♭ B♭
Glo - ry! glo - ry! Hal - le - lu - jah!
Glo - ry! glo - ry! Hal - le - lu - jah! His
E♭ B♭ F B♭
truth is march - ing on.

My Hope Is Built

F C C7
oth - er ground is sink - ing sand, All
F B♭ F C C7 F B♭ F
oth - er ground is sink - ing sand. A - men.

Choose Life

Text: Verses 1 & 2 - Matt. 25:35-41 (Adapted)

Music by Loretta Ellenberger

F
Dm
F
Choose life, oh choose!
gave me some drink. Na - ked and
give you some drink? When were you
on - go - ing soul. God - cen - tered
Dm
B♭
Dm
cold and you gave me clothes. When did I
na - ked and I gave you clothes? Do to the
free - dom through - out all of strife! Christ - love is
1, 2.
F
Dm
B♭
1, 2.
Dm
do these things for I knew not twas you!
least of these and you do un - to me.
in us, tell - ing us to choose.
1, 2.

3. Dm F B♭

Choose life ___ now! ___

3.

life! ___ Choose life ___

3.

B♭ Dm7 F

"Fol - low me." ___

now! ___ "Fol - low me." ___

Lord of the Dance

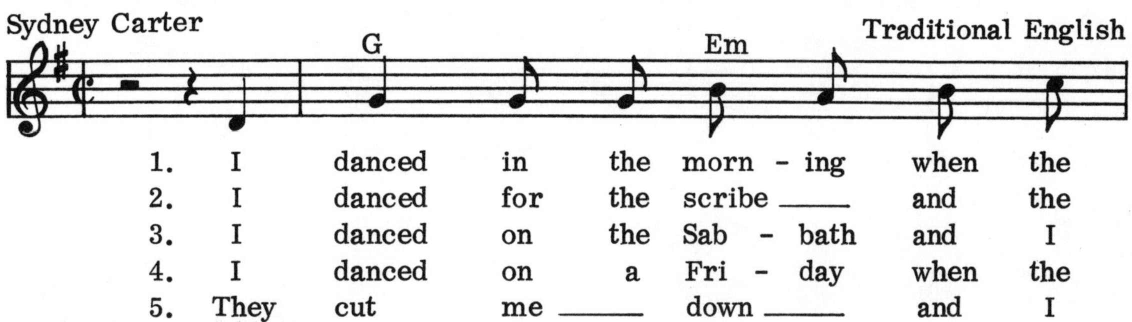

Bm Em Am C
earth was be - gun, And I danced in the moon and the
phar - i - see But they would not dance and they
cured the lame, The ho - ly peo - ple
sky turned black, It's hard to dance with the
leap up high, I am the dance that'll
Em7 D C Em
stars and the sun, And I came down from heav - en and I
wouldn't fol - low me. I danced for the fish - er - men, for
said it was a shame. They whipped and they stripped and they
dev - il on your back. They bur - ied my bod - y and they
nev - er, nev - er die. I'll live in you if you'll
Bm Em Am D
danced on the earth. At Beth - le - hem I
James and John. They came with me and the
hung me high, And they left me there on a
thought I'd gone. But I am the dance and I
live in me. I am the Lord of the
G C G Chorus G Bm Em
had my birth.
dance went on.
cross to die. Dance then wher - ev - er you may be.
still go on.
Dance, said he.
G Bm Am7 D G Em
I am the Lord of the Dance said he And I'll lead you all wher -
G Bm Am7 D
ev - er you may be, And I'll lead you all in the
1, 2, 3, 4.
G C G
last time
G C G
Dance said he. Dance said he.

New Life

Bill Comeau | Ed Summerlin

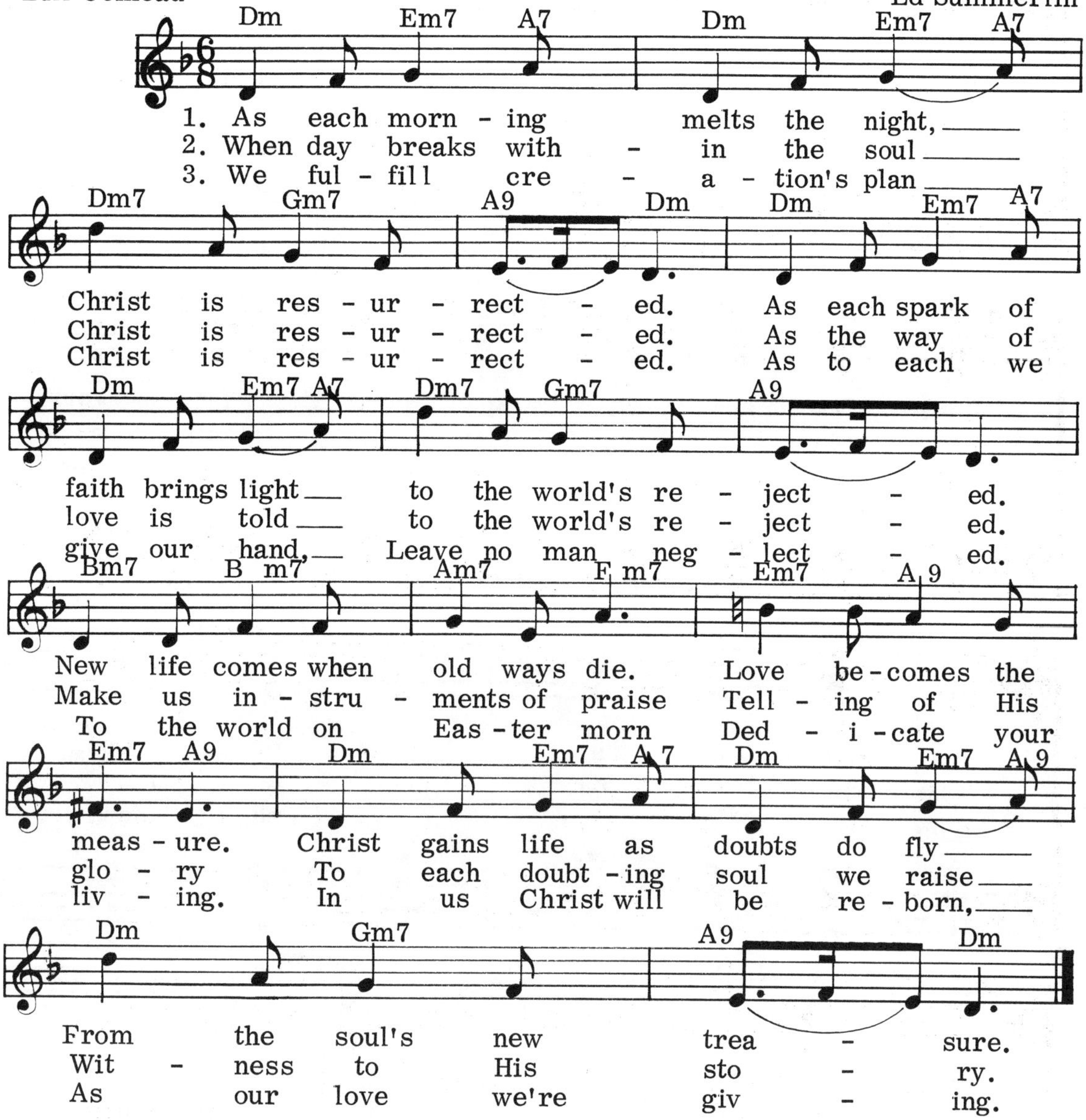
Dm Em7 A7 Dm Em7 A7
1. As each morn - ing melts the night,
2. When day breaks with - in the soul
3. We ful - fill cre - a - tion's plan
Dm7 Gm7 A9 Dm Dm Em7 A7
Christ is res - ur - rect - ed. As each spark of
Christ is res - ur - rect - ed. As the way of
Christ is res - ur - rect - ed. As to each we
Dm Em7 A7 Dm7 Gm7 A9
faith brings light to the world's re - ject - ed.
love is told to the world's re - ject - ed.
give our hand, Leave no man neg - lect - ed.
Bm7 B m7 Am7 F m7 Em7 A 9
New life comes when old ways die. Love be - comes the
Make us in - stru - ments of praise Tell - ing of His
To the world on Eas - ter morn Ded - i - cate your
Em7 A9 Dm Em7 A7 Dm Em7 A9
meas - ure. Christ gains life as doubts do fly
glo - ry To each doubt - ing soul we raise
liv - ing. In us Christ will be re - born,
Dm Gm7 A9 Dm
From the soul's new trea - sure.
Wit - ness to His sto - ry.
As our love we're giv - ing.

A Place to Stand

David J. Randolph | John Zundel

1. In a time of fier - y tri - als
2. We have seen the world grow small - er
3. Let the church, Lord, be your peo - ple

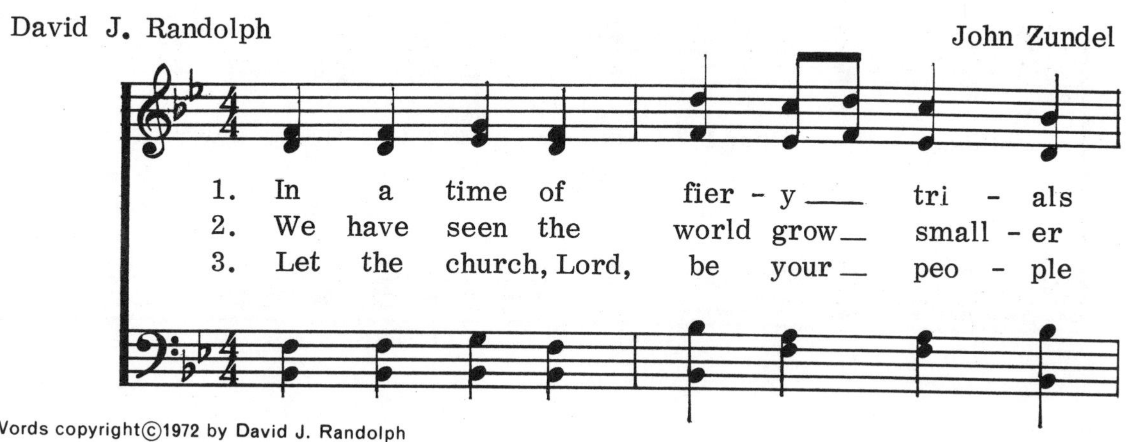

Trou - bles set on ev - ery hand;
Walked the moon and brushed the stars,
Pure of heart and clean of hand,
Lord, we ask no spec - ial fa - vors,
Yet on earth we stand no tall - er
Till the world in ad - o - ra - tion
Just give us a place to stand.
Than our guns and pris - on bars.
Hum - bly at your cross shall stand.
Place to stand a - gainst temp - ta - tion,
Lord, lift us to our full stat - ure,
Cleanse us Lord of low am - bi - tion,
Place to stand a - gainst the foe,
Help us on our feet to stand,
Let our dream for you be grand.

Place to stand in prayer and wit - ness,
Leave be - hind our beast - ly rap - ture
Bring us from our low con - di - tion
Till a - cross the world we go.
March in time to your com - mand.
To your side, a place to stand. A - men.

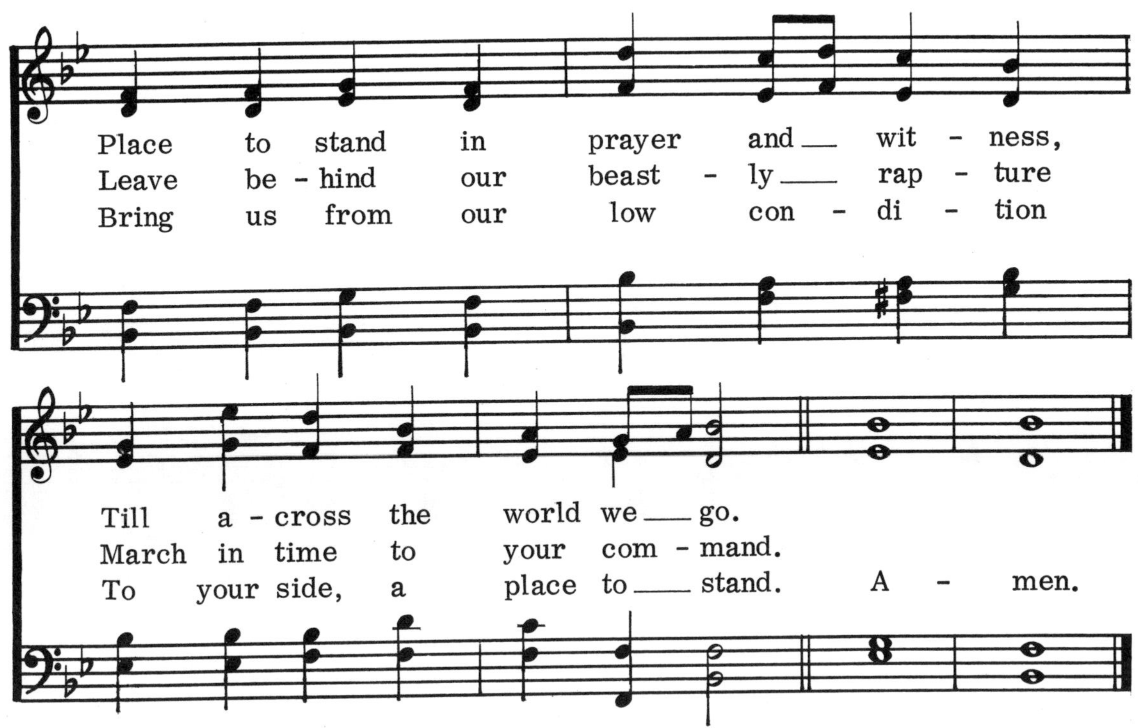

The Road of Life

Words and music by Jim Moore

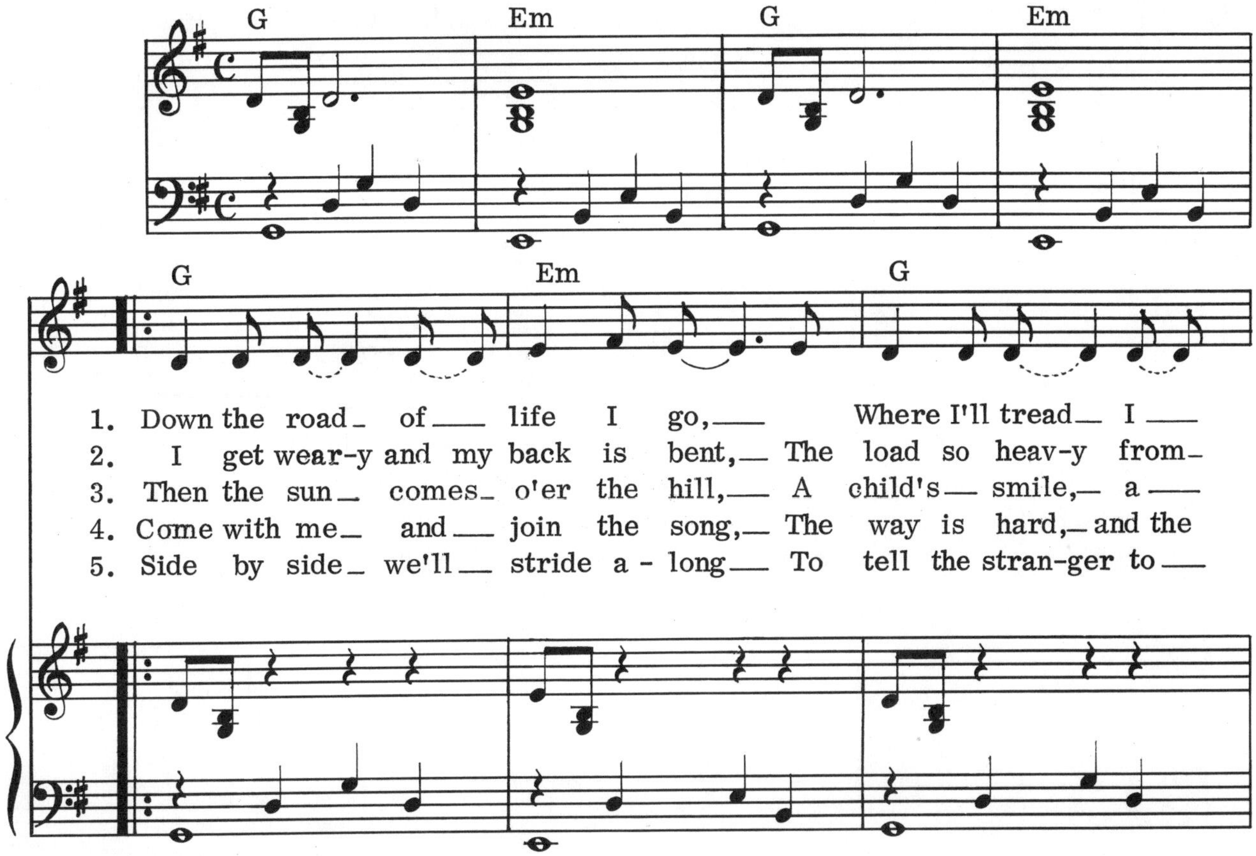
G
Em
G
Em
G
Em
G
1. Down the road of life I go, Where I'll tread I
2. I get wear-y and my back is bent, The load so heav-y from
3. Then the sun comes o'er the hill, A child's smile, a
4. Come with me and join the song, The way is hard, and the
5. Side by side we'll stride a - long To tell the stran-ger to

Em
G
Em
do not know, But wher - e'er I look my God is stand - ing
dis-con-tent I know he's right, but I can't get on my
daf-fo - dil, A bird's sweet song and dew that lasts all
road is long, The threat so great that you can hard - ly
tell the throng, And all the earth the mes-sage of his
Am
there Call - ing
way. Deep des -
day. Take me,
dare. But he needs
love. We'll help men
me, "Snap out of your rev - er - ie! The
pair, the tear-drops they fill the air. No
Lord! Life's worth the liv - ing for! I'll
you, his work with man-kind to do. A
stand in the midst of a trou-bled land. God's

B7
time is soon and most of the world don't care."
winds to drive the storm clouds of life a - way.
sing my song till no one can turn a - way.
lone - ly world is cry - ing for you to care.
will be done on earth as in heaven a - bove.
Em
1,2,3,4.
5.
Thy
Am
B7
Em
will be done. Thy
Am
B7
Em
Am
E
will be done!

Stir up Thy Mighty Men

"Let us consider how to stir up one another to love and good works" (Hebrews 10:24)

"He stirs up the people" (Luke 23:5)

"Stir up the mighty men" (Joel 3:9)

C A7 D G D G7
men, Stir up Thy might-y men, Stir
C F C F E Am F G C
up Thy might-y men the way He stirred them up.

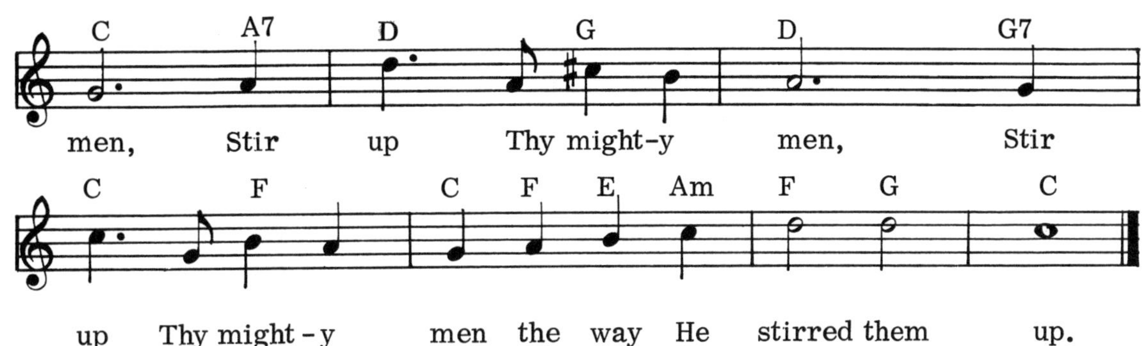

What's That I Hear

Moderately

Phil Ochs

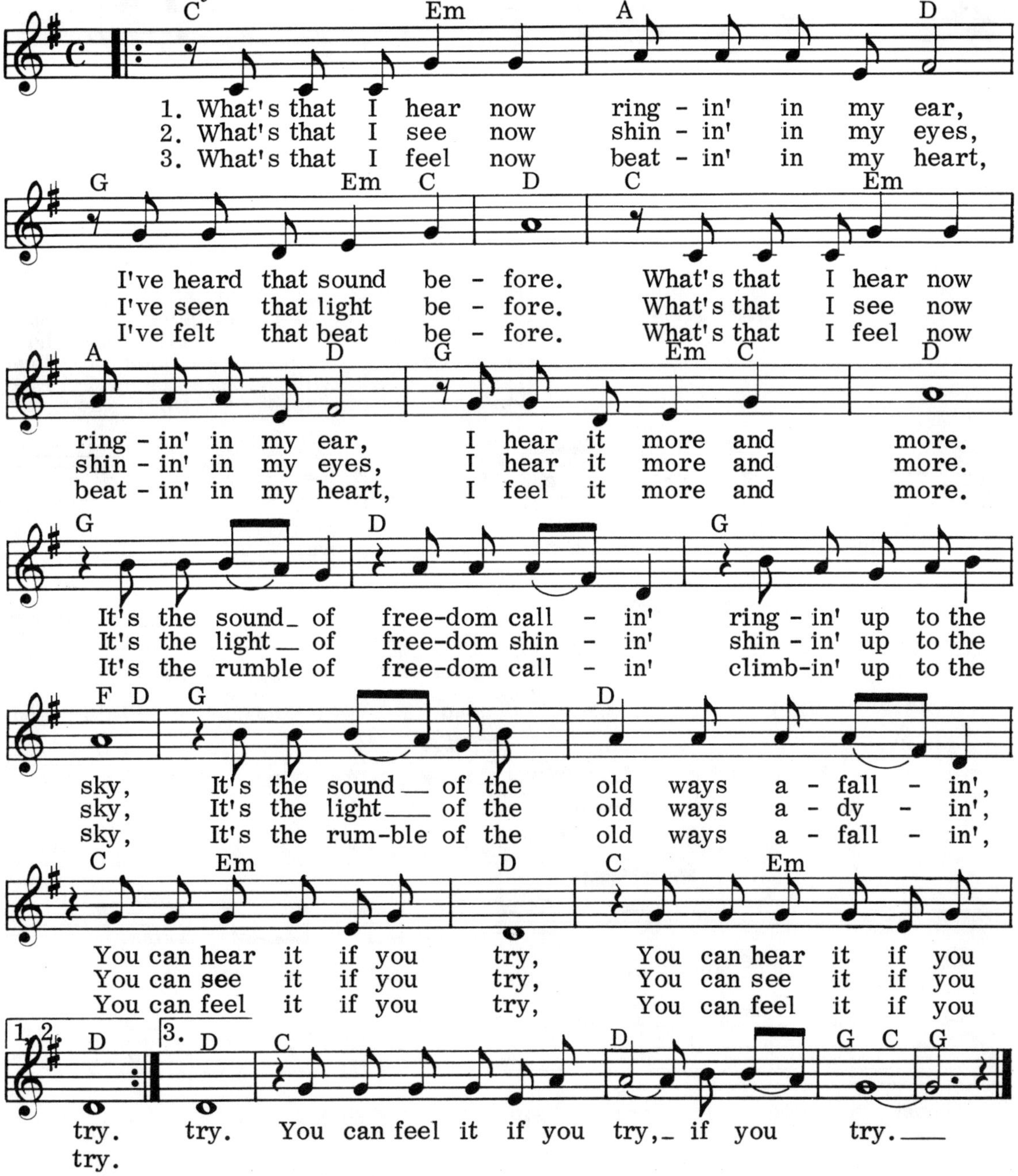
C Em A D
1. What's that I hear now ring-in' in my ear,
2. What's that I see now shin-in' in my eyes,
3. What's that I feel now beat-in' in my heart,
G Em C D C Em
I've heard that sound be-fore. What's that I hear now
I've seen that light be-fore. What's that I see now
I've felt that beat be-fore. What's that I feel now
A D G Em C D
ring-in' in my ear, I hear it more and more.
shin-in' in my eyes, I hear it more and more.
beat-in' in my heart, I feel it more and more.
G D G
It's the sound_ of free-dom call-in' ring-in' up to the
It's the light_ of free-dom shin-in' shin-in' up to the
It's the rumble of free-dom call-in' climb-in' up to the
F D G D
sky, It's the sound_ of the old ways a-fall-in',
sky, It's the light_ of the old ways a-dy-in',
sky, It's the rum-ble of the old ways a-fall-in',
C Em D C Em
You can hear it if you try, You can hear it if you
You can see it if you try, You can see it if you
You can feel it if you try, You can feel it if you
1.2. D 3. D C D G C G
try. try. You can feel it if you try,_ if you try._
try.

Down by the Riverside

Foster the Spirit of Francis of Assisi

Bill Garrett
Ed. and Arr. by Robert O. Hoffelt

Lively ♩ = 120 *in strict rhythm*

f-mf

F / B♭ / C7 / F / B♭ / C7 / F / B♭ / Bdim7
Foster the spirit of Francis of Assisi; Foster the spirit of Francis of Assisi; make me an instrument of thy peace.

C / C / F / C7
Where there is hatred, let me sow

to 𝄋 *after second time*
F 𝄐
love;

(change chords on repeats)
freely *mp*

F / Dm / A — C7 / B♭ / Gm — F / Bdim / G7

where in-jury, par-don, where dis-cord,
where doubt, faith; where de-spair,
where dark-ness, light; where sad-ness,

God Give Us Your Peace

Phil West

Ed Summerlin

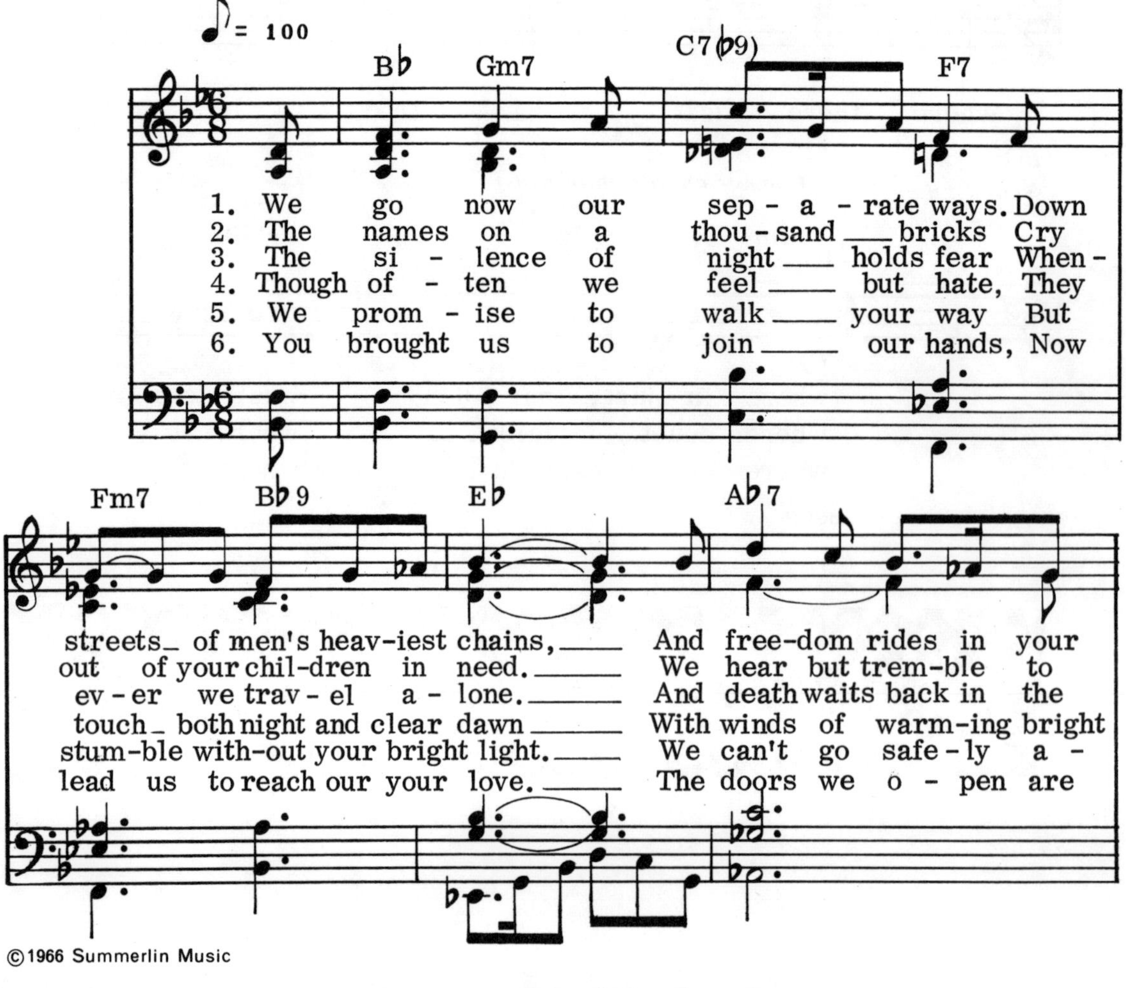

♪ = 100

B♭ Gm7 C7(♭9) F7

1. We go now our sep - a - rate ways. Down
2. The names on a thou - sand bricks Cry
3. The si - lence of night holds fear When -
4. Though of - ten we feel but hate, They
5. We prom - ise to walk your way But
6. You brought us to join our hands, Now

Fm7 B♭9 E♭ A♭7

streets of men's heav-iest chains, And free-dom rides in your
out of your chil-dren in need. We hear but trem-ble to
ev - er we trav - el a - lone. And death waits back in the
touch both night and clear dawn With winds of warm-ing bright
stum-ble with-out your bright light. We can't go safe - ly a -
lead us to reach our your love. The doors we o - pen are

Last Night I Had the Strangest Dream

Simply, with dignity

Ed McCurdy

C C7 F

1. Last night I had the strang - est dream I ev - er had be -
2. And when the pa - per was all signed, And a mil - lion cop - ies
3. Last night I had the strang - est dream I ev - er had be -

simile

C G7
fore, I dreamed the world had
made, They all joined hands and
fore, I dreamed the world had
C Am Dm(or G7) G7
all a - greed, to put an end to
cir - cled 'round, And grate - ful prayers were
all a - greed, to put an end to
C Fine Dm(or F)
war. I dreamed there
made. And the peo - ple
war.
THE WAR IS ENDED!

F
C
G7
was a might - y room, And the room was
on the streets be - low Were dan - cing
C
C7
F
filled with men, And the pa - per
'round and 'round. With swords and
C
Am
they were sign - ing said they'd
guns and u - ni - forms all
G7
C (or G7)
C
D.C. al Fine
nev-er fight a - gain.
scat-tered on the ground.

Peace

Words and music by
W. T. Holland, Jr.

Dm7
E
man - kind we see. Men are
yearn - ing to find. Men will
Am
E
Am
C
F
full of hate But it's not too late To
nev - er cease Their quest for peace 'Til they
Am
CM7
D7
G7
C7
show what man - kind yet may be.
search in their own heart and mind.
=120
F6
Gm7
C7
mf
1. No peace in pre - tend - ing There's har - mo - ny on
2. No peace in pre - tend - ing That things change o - ver
3. No peace in pre - tend - ing That all man-kind is

F F6 Gm7
earth. Some peace in con - tend - ing There
night. Some peace in con - tend - ing Takes
just. Some peace in con - tend - ing To
C7 F Dm F
ff
still is room for mirth; For the world goes
time to make things right; For the world goes
this we can ad - just; For the world goes
Dm F F6
mf
on, It's been go-ing on a ver-y long time. Real peace is re -
on, It's been go-ing on a ver-y long time. Real peace is re -
on, It's been go-ing on a ver-y long time. Real peace is re -

Gm7 C7 1. F 2. F D. S.

mem-bring — Man - kind can find re - birth. light.
mem-bring — Through dark - ness comes the
mem-bring — In God each man must

3. F Bb F

trust.

mf p pp

(Repeat phrase "Real peace is remembring, In God each man must trust." in final verse) (Optional)

Shalom, Chaverim

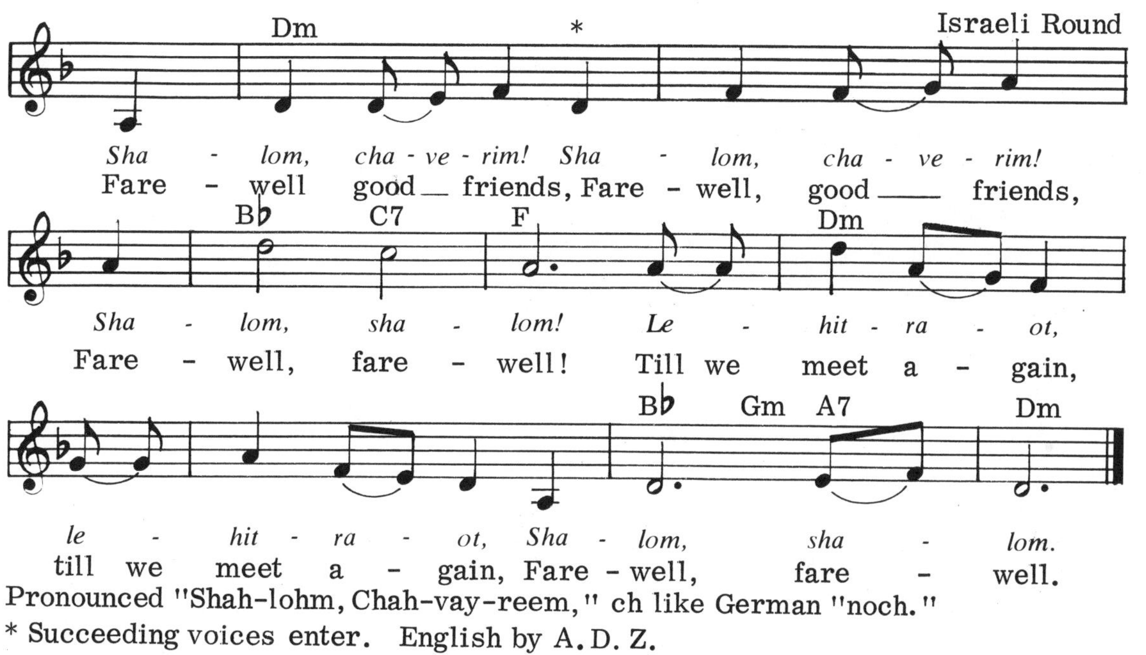

From 101 Rounds

Where Have All the Flowers Gone

Pete Seeger

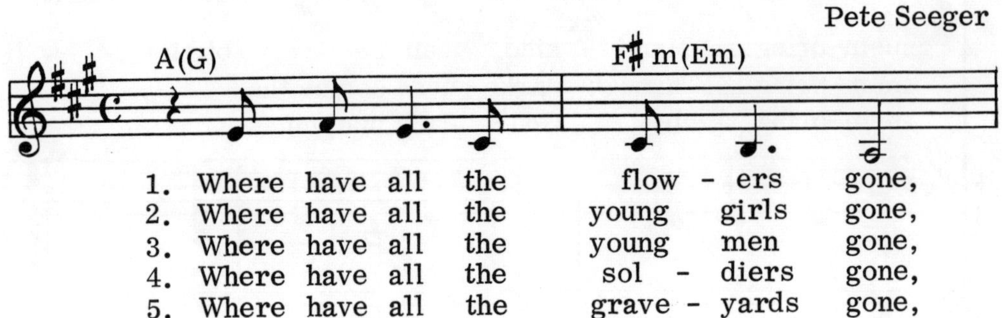

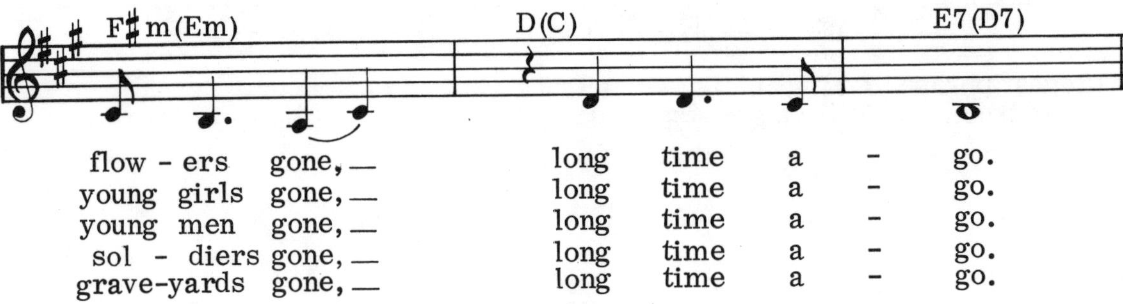

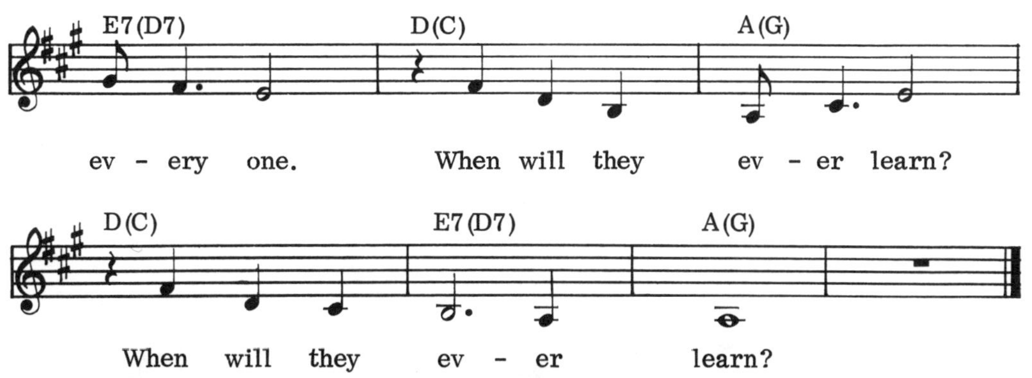

I Want Justice

Paraphrase of Amos

Words and music by Jim Moore

From *Songs by Dust and Ashes*

COMMITMENT LOVE AND JUSTICE

F
Am
Dm
proph - et's son am I I'm just a lone - ly
Am
E
Am
shep - herd who hears the lamb - kin's cry. I
G
F
do not wear the cloth, I'm not God's man by

Am
Dm
Am
trade. I dress the loft - y syc-a - more, and
E
Am
'tis for that I'm paid. But the li - on has
E
Am
roared, who shall not fear? The Lord God has

E
Am
spo - ken, who can but speak? Now
F
Dm7
there - fore hear his word. I
Dm C Dm C Dm
hate and de-spise all your pot-lucks, your sol-emn as-sem-blies in church. Your
prayers are as emp-ty as des - erts; your hymns are all noise, not a search. You
Em D Em D Em
drink wine from bowls, not in jig-gers; you eat of the calf not the bull. You
buy off the poor with your dol-lars, and sell the need-y for shoes. I want

Am
Em
jus - tice! Jus - tice! like free flow - ing wat - ers, and
Am
Em
Righ - teous-ness! Righ - teous - ness! like cas - cad - ing streams. Love,
F
Em
F
E
good-ness, re-ject not the need-y, — the ghet - to is not the Lord's dream! But
F
Am
you have turned jus - tice to poi - son, — and

F
Am
giv - en the fruit to the worm. You
F
G
lie on your beds of white ivo - ry while the
F
E
beds of the poor you would burn. I want
Am
Em
Jus - tice! Jus - tice! like free flow - ing wat - ers, and

JUSTICE
Am
Em
Righ - teous-ness! Righ - teous-ness! like cas - cad - ing streams. Love
F
Em
good - ness, re - ject not the need - y, the
F
E
F
rit.
Dm7
E
ghet-to is not the Lord's dream. Let jus - tice flow down like a stream!

The Lord's Vineyard

Paraphrase of
Isaiah 5:1-7

Words and music
James Moore

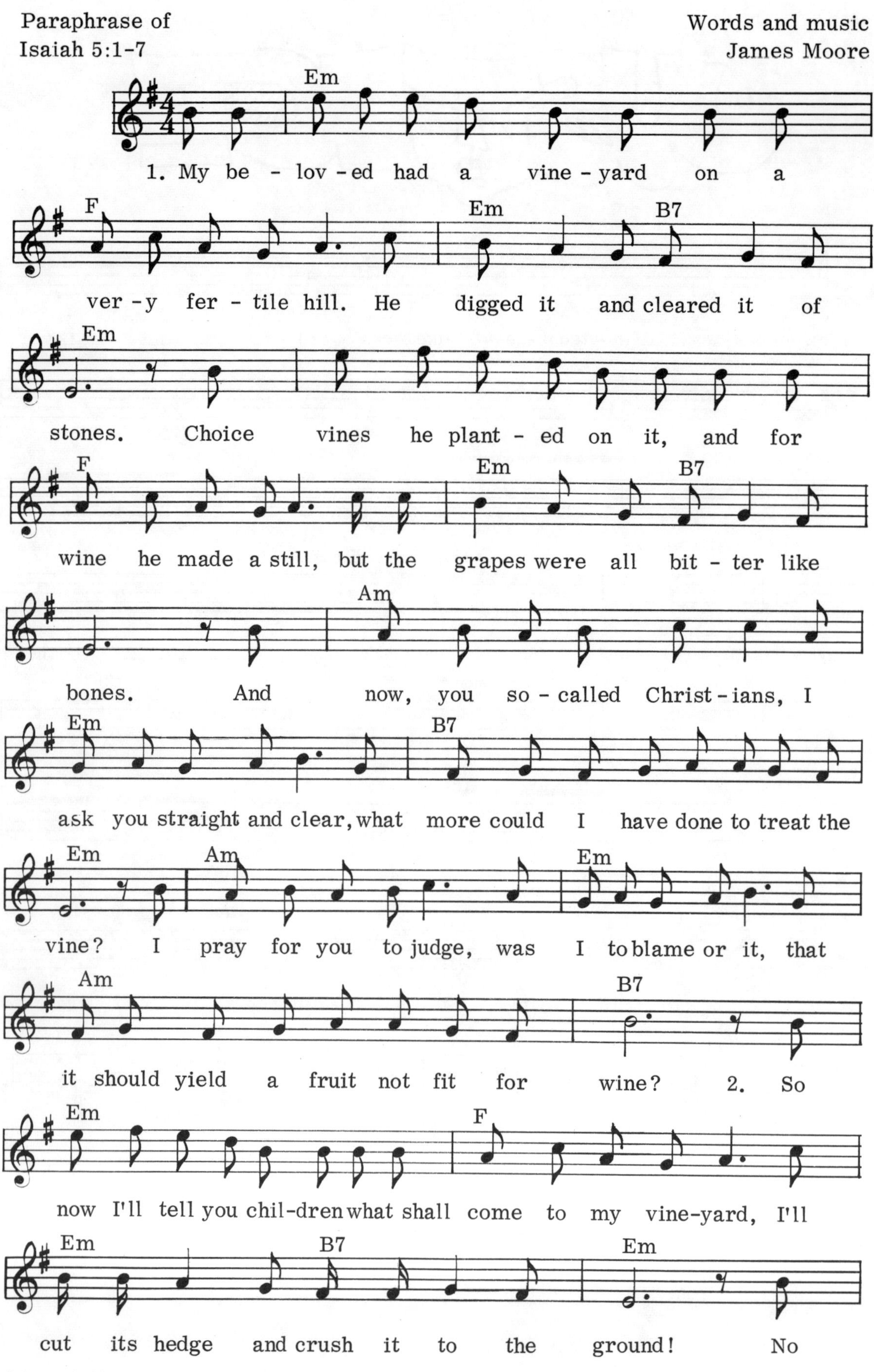

F
love will come un-to it, on-ly bri - ars and sharp thorns. The
Em B7 Em
clouds will not drop rain, no drink be found. For the
Am Em
vine-yard of the Lord is the house you call the church, and the
Am B7
men of God were once his pleas - ant plant - ing. But
Em F
when he looked for jus - tice, be - hold, he saw blood-shed, and for
Em rit. B7 Em
righ - teous - ness, be - hold, he heard a cry.

Love Come A-Tricklin' Down

The Raddle of Love

Were You There?

Spiritual

What Wondrous Love Is This

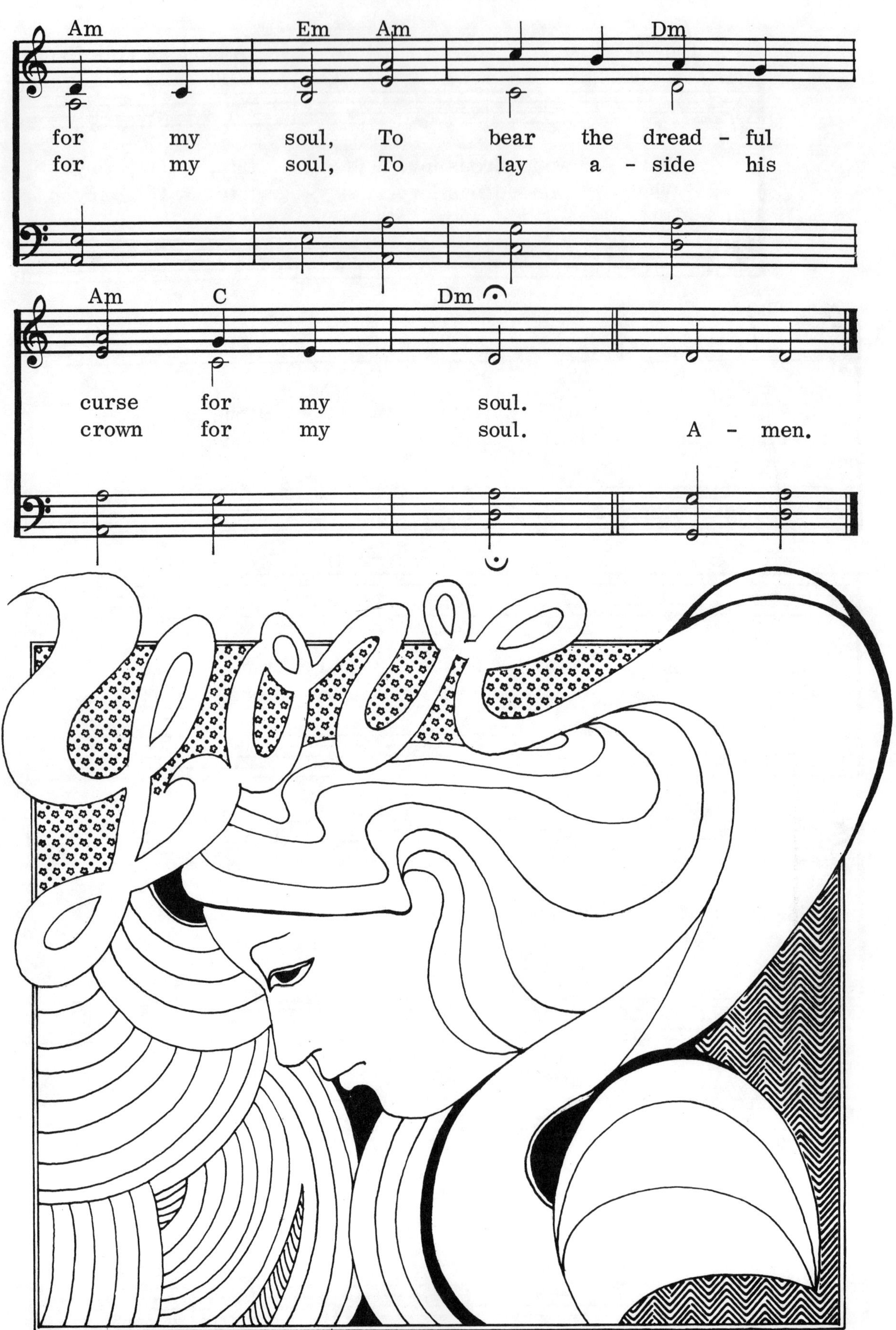
Am Em Am Dm
for my soul, To bear the dread - ful
for my soul, To lay a - side his
Am C Dm
curse for my soul.
crown for my soul. A - men.
Love

All My Trials

Traditional

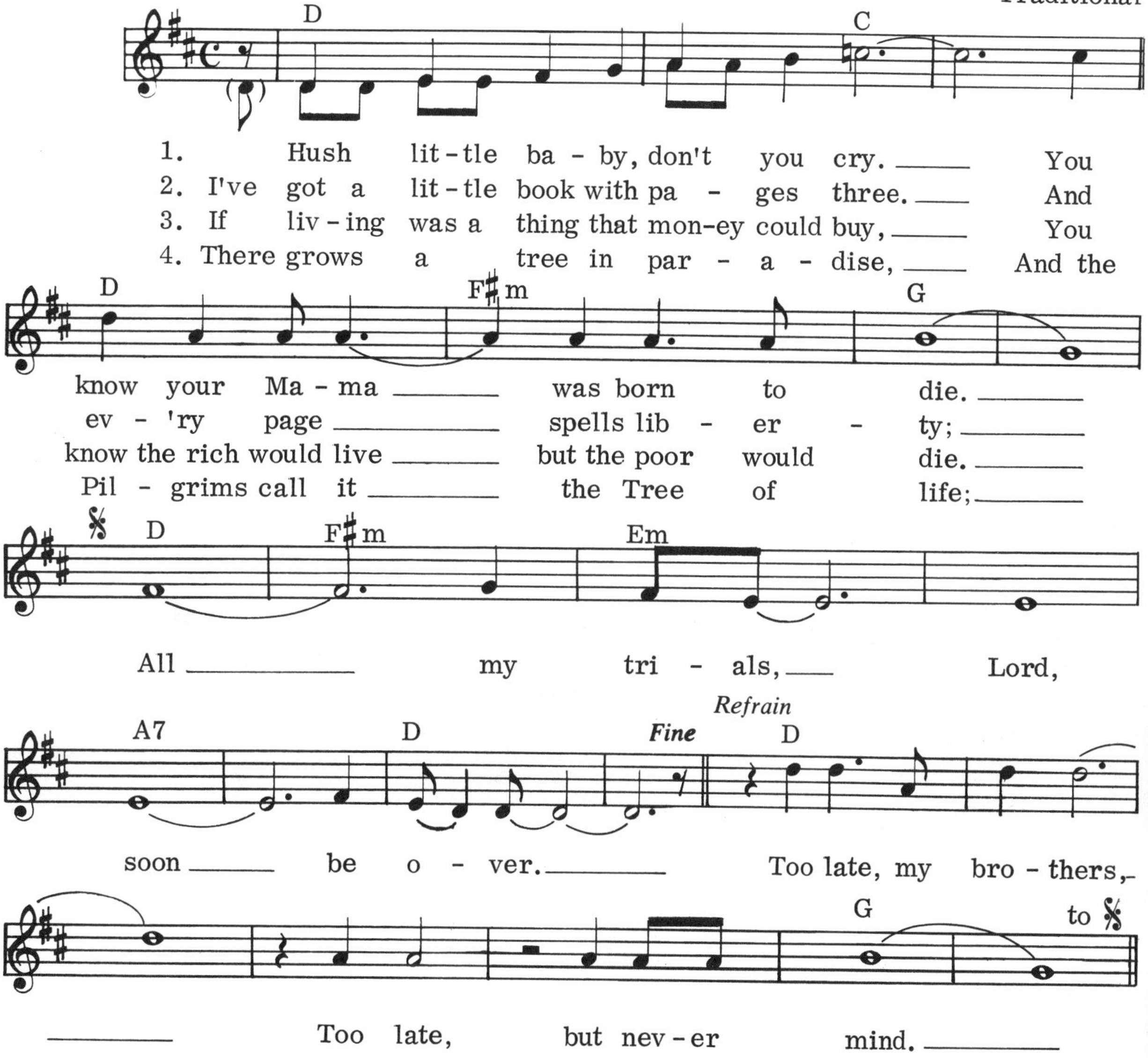

D C
1. Hush lit-tle ba-by, don't you cry. ___ You
2. I've got a lit-tle book with pa - ges three. ___ And
3. If liv-ing was a thing that mon-ey could buy, ___ You
4. There grows a tree in par - a - dise, ___ And the
D F♯m G
know your Ma-ma ___ was born to die. ___
ev - 'ry page ___ spells lib - er - ty; ___
know the rich would live ___ but the poor would die. ___
Pil - grims call it ___ the Tree of life; ___
D F♯m Em
All ___ my tri - als, ___ Lord,
A7 D Fine Refrain D
soon ___ be o - ver. ___ Too late, my bro - thers, ___
G to 𝄋
Too late, but nev-er mind. ___

Amazing Grace

John Newton and
John P. Rees (ascribed)

Early American

G
1. A - maz - ing ___ grace! how
2. 'Twas grace that ___ taught my
3. Through man - y ___ dan - gers,
4. When we've been ___ there ten

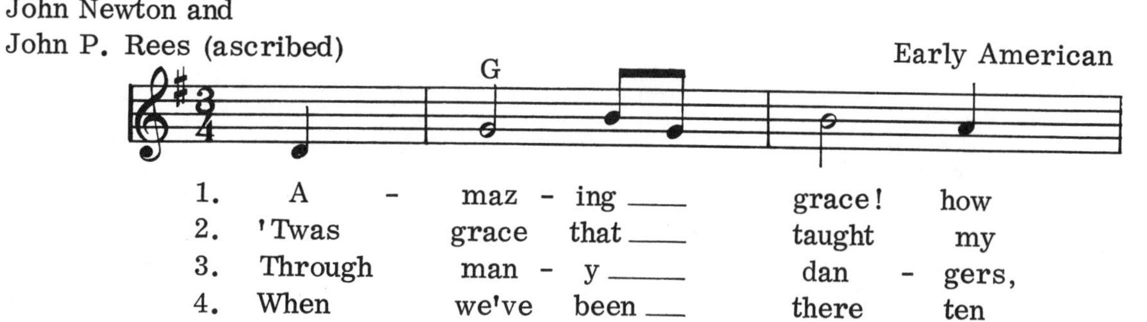

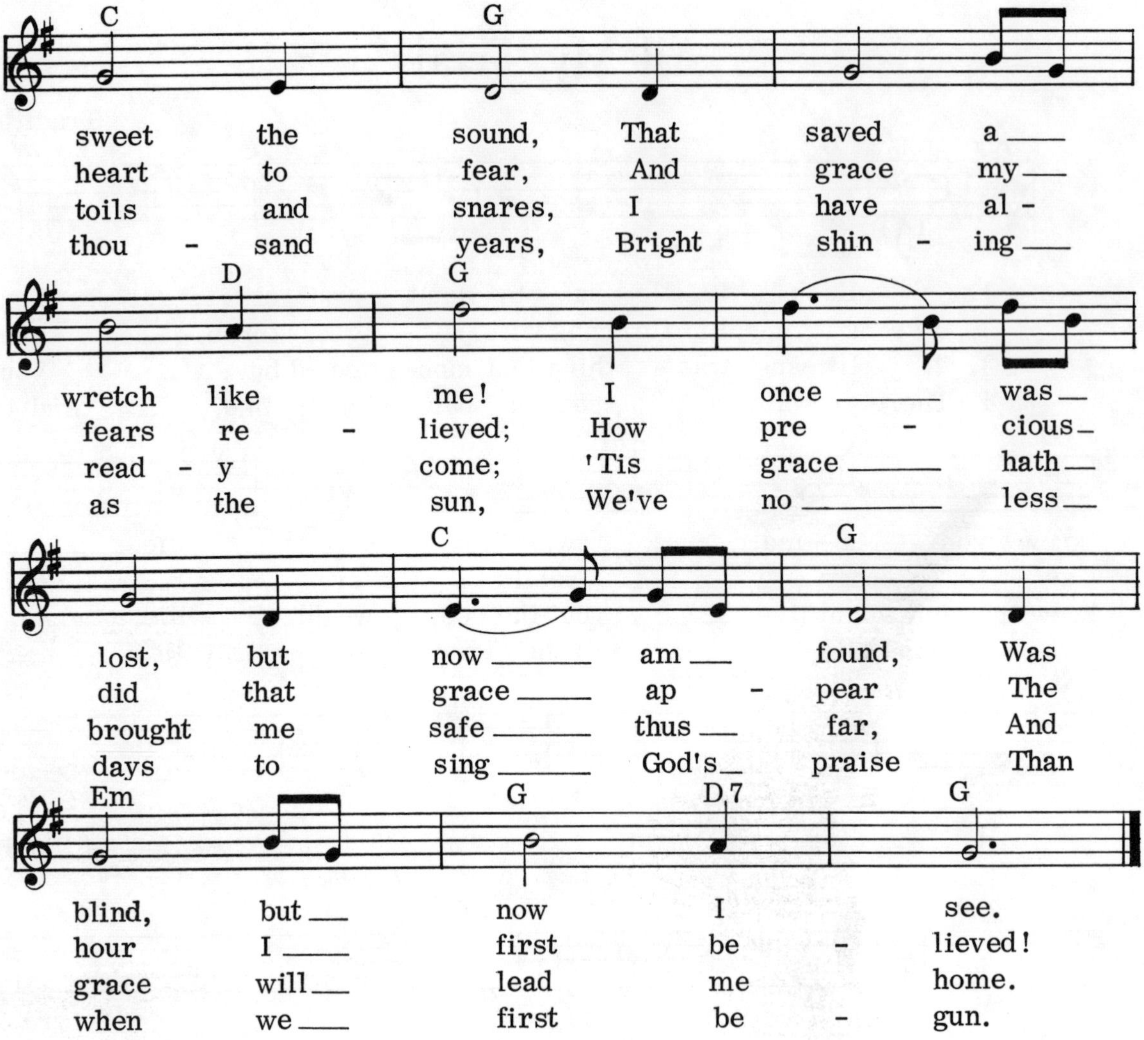

C G
sweet the sound, That saved a
heart to fear, And grace my
toils and snares, I have al -
thou - sand years, Bright shin - ing
D G
wretch like me! I once was
fears re - lieved; How pre - cious
read - y come; 'Tis grace hath
as the sun, We've no less
C G
lost, but now am found, Was
did that grace ap - pear The
brought me safe thus far, And
days to sing God's praise Than
Em G D7 G
blind, but now I see.
hour I first be - lieved!
grace will lead me home.
when we first be - gun.

Everything Is Beautiful

Moderately bright
Ray Stevens
F B♭ F
Je - sus loves the lit - tle chil - dren,
mf
3

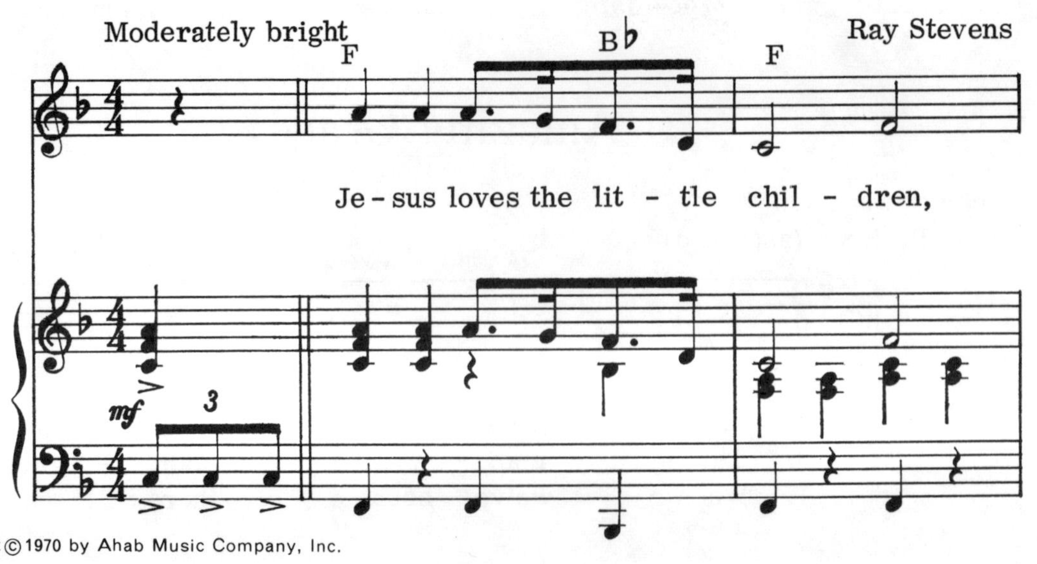

C
F
C
all the lit - tle chil-dren of the world, Red and
F
B♭
F
yel - low, black and white, they are pre-cious in His sight. Je - sus
B♭
C7
F
loves the lit - tle chil - dren of the world.
Chorus
Ev - ery-thing is
F
beau - ti - ful

Dm7
G7sus
G7
in its own way,
Like a star-ry
Csus
C
Csus
C
F
B♭
sum - mer night, or a snow-cov-ered win - ter's day.
F
Dm7
Ev - ery-bod-y's beau - ti - ful in their own
G7sus
G7
Csus
C
way,
un - der God's hea - ven the

Csus
C
F
B♭
F
C7
world's gon-na find ___ a way. ___
F
Verse
C
B♭
1. There is none so blind ___ as he who will not
F
C
see. ___ We must not close our minds, ___ We must
B♭
F
let our thoughts be free, ___ for ev-'ry hour

C
B♭
that pas-ses by
you know the world gets a lit - tle bit
F
old - er.
It's time to re-al - ize
C
B♭
that beau-ty lies in the eyes of the be -

1.

F Bb F

hold - er. And ev - ery - thing is

2.

D.S. and fade out on chorus

F Bb F

hold - er. Ev - ery - thing is

Verse 2: We shouldn't care about the length of his hair or the color of his skin
Don't worry about what shows from without but the love that lives within
We gonna get it all together now and everything gonna work out fine
Just take a little time to look on the good side my friend and straighten it out in your mind.

Joy Is Now

Words and Music by Anne and Phil West

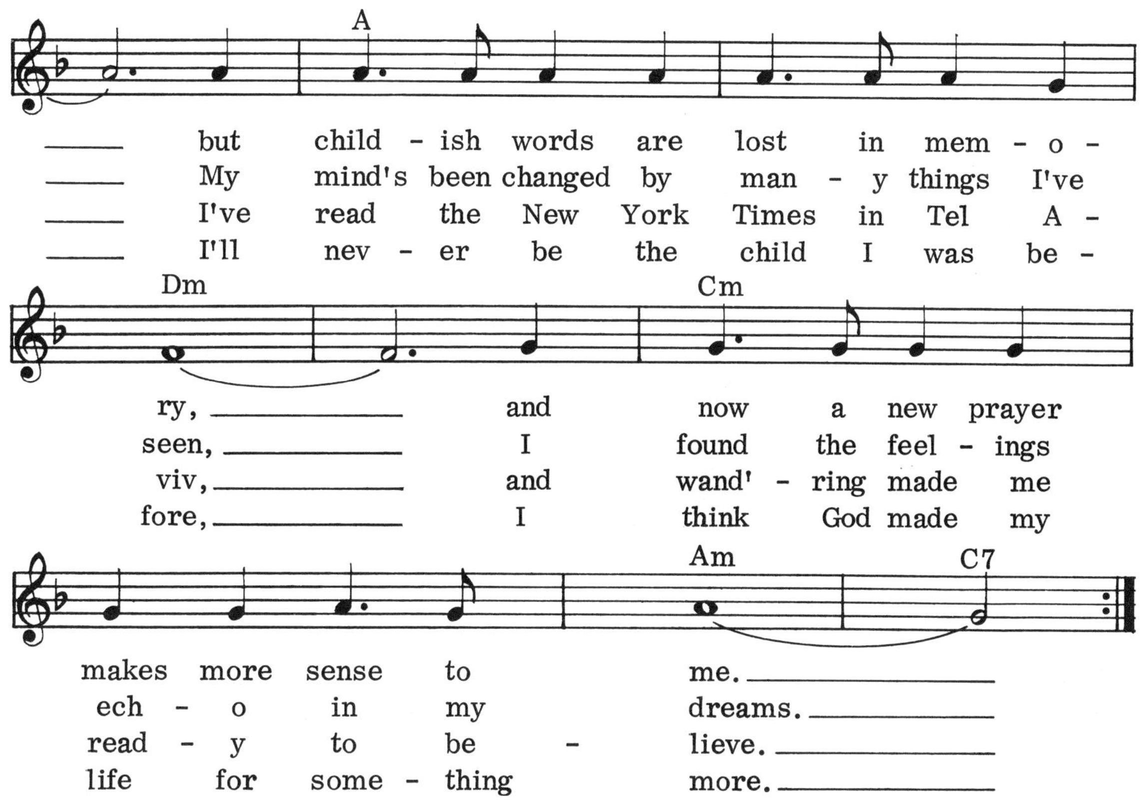

O Freedom

John A. and Alan Lomax

Charles and Ruth Seeger

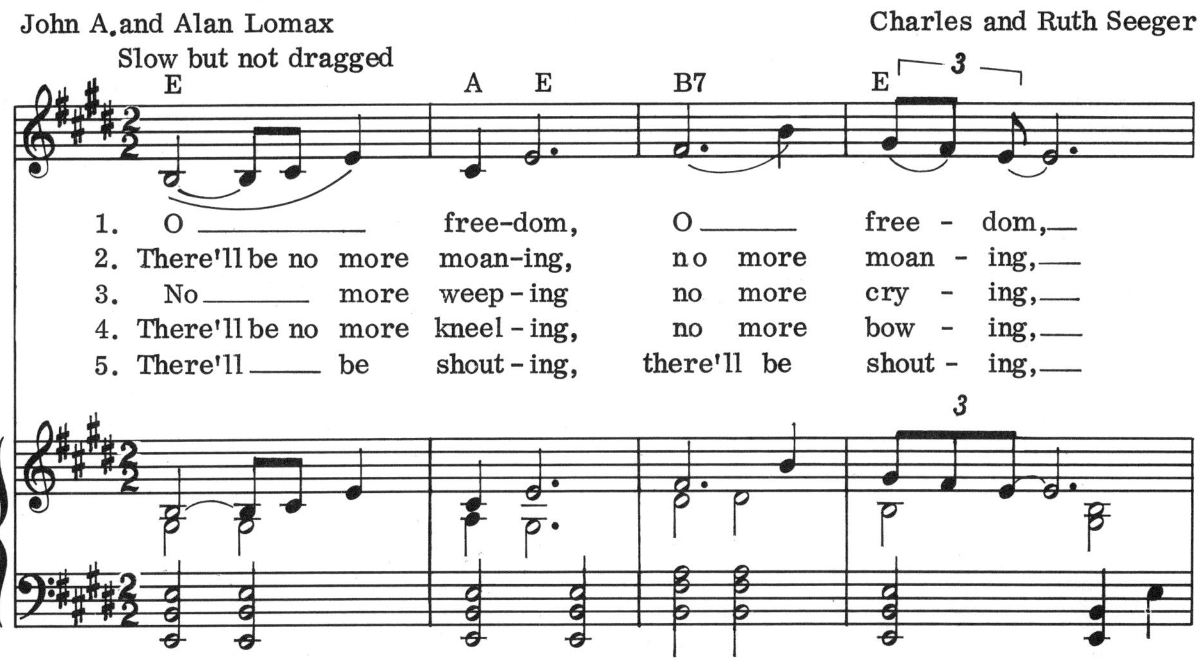

A E
B7
O ___ freedom after a while, ___
No ___ more moaning after a while, ___
No ___ more weeping after a while, ___
No ___ more kneeling after a while, ___
There'll be shouting after a while, ___
A E A7
And before I'd be a slave, ___ I'd be
And before I'd be a slave, ___ I'd be
And before I'd be a slave, ___ I'd be
And before I'd be a slave, ___ I'd be
And before I'd be a slave, ___ I'd be
A E
buried in my grave, And go home, ___ to my
buried in my grave, And go home, ___ to my
buried in my grave, And go home, ___ to my
buried in my grave, And go home, ___ to my
buried in my grave, And go home, ___ to my

3
B7
E
Fine
Lord and be free.
Lord and be free.
Lord and be free.
Lord and be free.
Lord and be free.
2. There'll be
3
3

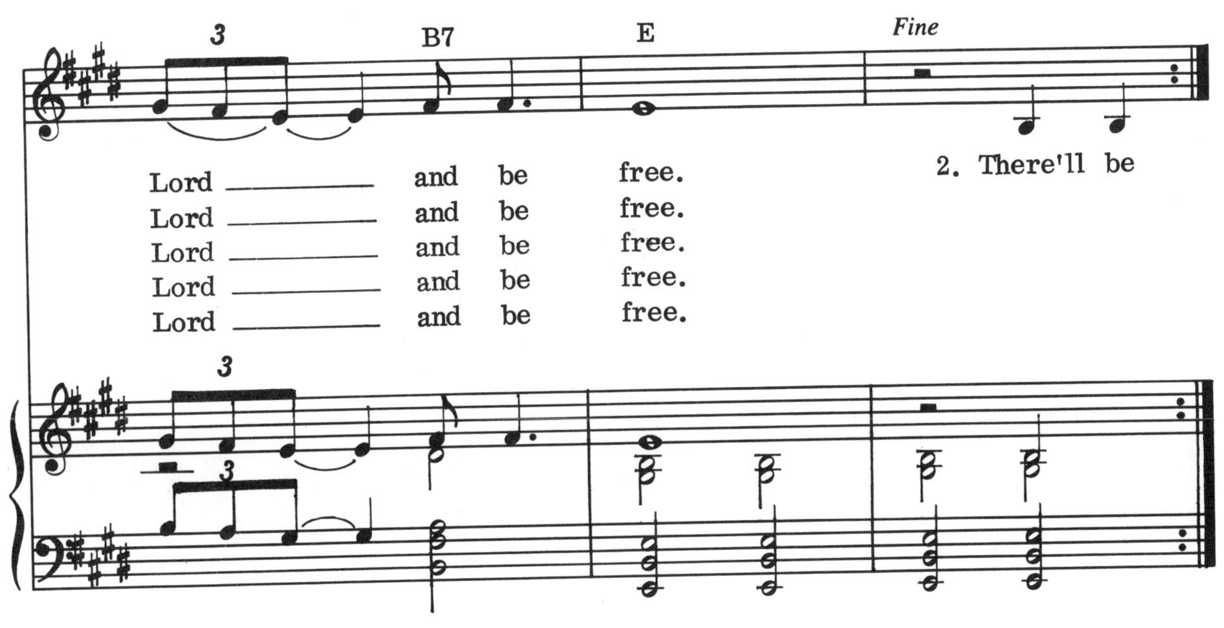

Simple Gifts

Traditional

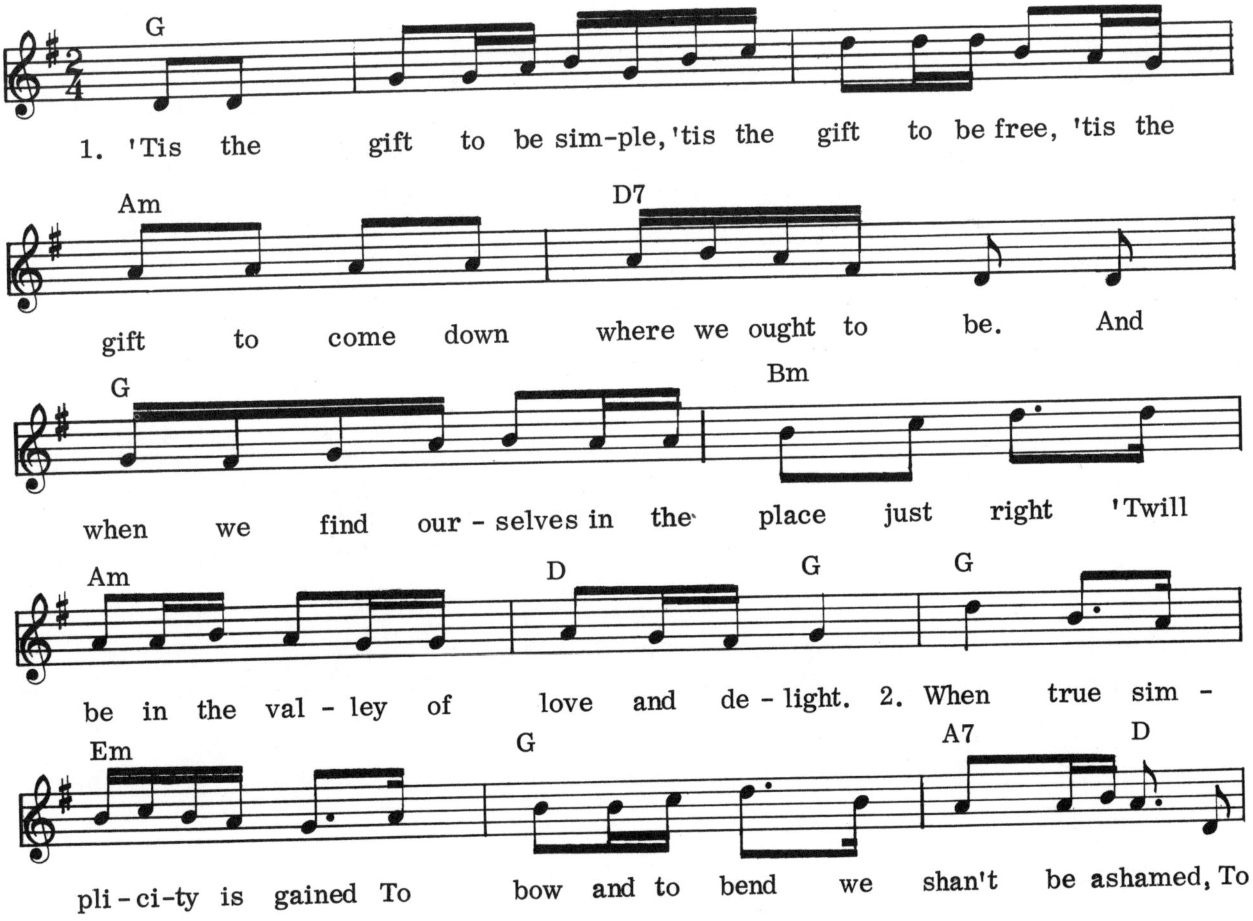
G
1. 'Tis the gift to be sim-ple, 'tis the gift to be free, 'tis the
Am
D7
gift to come down where we ought to be. And
G
Bm
when we find our - selves in the place just right 'Twill
Am
D
G
G
be in the val - ley of love and de - light. 2. When true sim -
Em
G
A7
D
pli - ci - ty is gained To bow and to bend we shan't be ashamed, To

G
turn, turn, will be our de - light, 'Til by
Am D7 G C G
turn - ing, turn - ing we come round right.

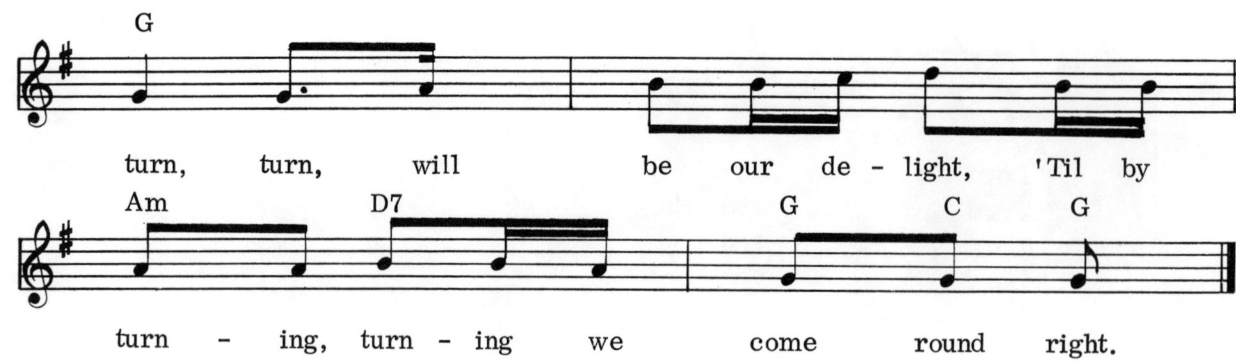

We Shall Overcome

Traditional

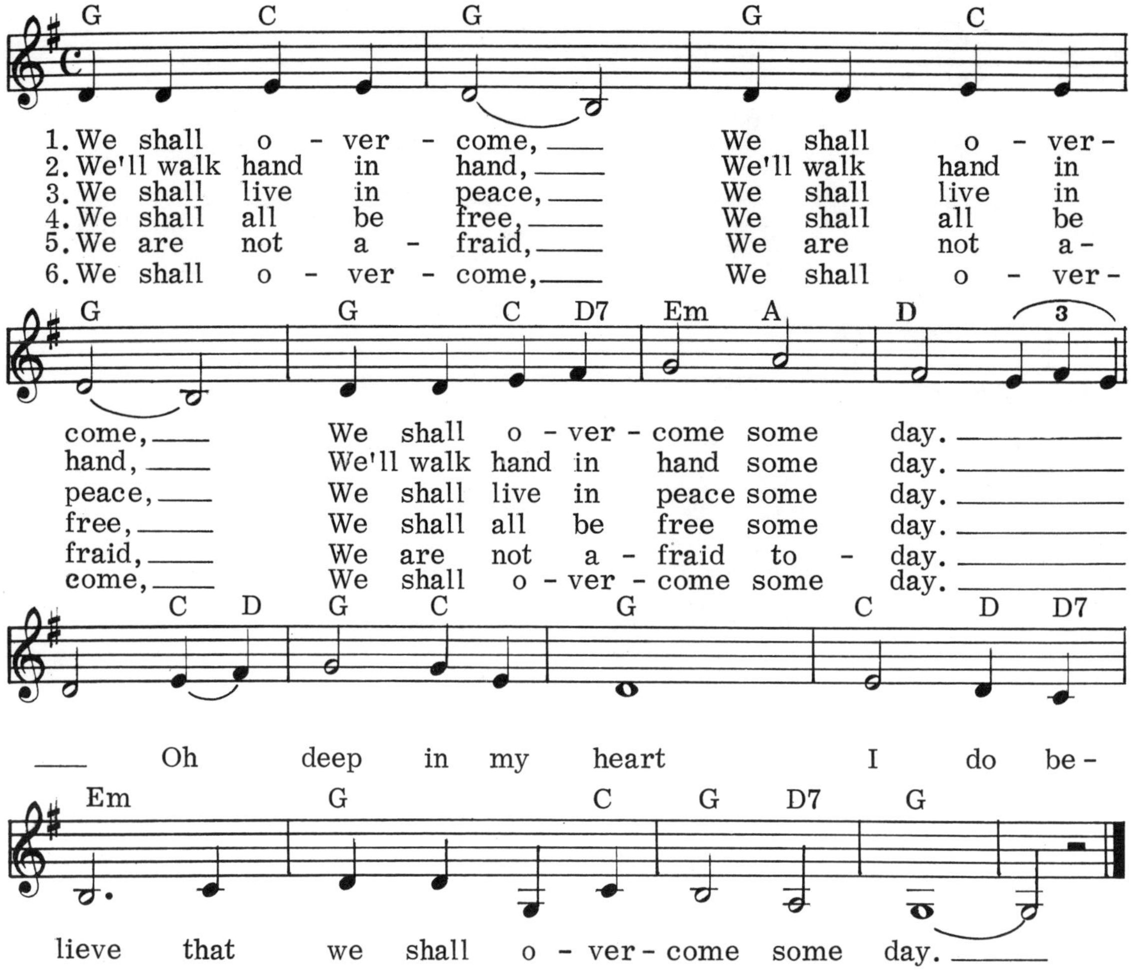
G C G G C
1. We shall o - ver - come, We shall o - ver -
2. We'll walk hand in hand, We'll walk hand in
3. We shall live in peace, We shall live in
4. We shall all be free, We shall all be
5. We are not a - fraid, We are not a -
6. We shall o - ver - come, We shall o - ver -
G G C D7 Em A D
3
come, We shall o - ver - come some day.
hand, We'll walk hand in hand some day.
peace, We shall live in peace some day.
free, We shall all be free some day.
fraid, We are not a - fraid to - day.
come, We shall o - ver - come some day.
C D G C G C D D7
Oh deep in my heart I do be -
Em G C G D7 G
lieve that we shall o - ver - come some day.

Bless the Lord

From *The Hymnal for Young Christians*
by permission of Clarence Rivers.

G6 Em A7 D7 G6 Em
Bless the Lord, you nights and days. 6. Light - nings and clouds,
G6 Em G6 Em A7 D7
bless the Lord. Bless the Lord, you winds of heav - en.
G6 Em G6 Em G6 Em
7. Now let the earth bless the Lord. Praise and glo - ri - fy
A7 D7 G6 Em G6 Em G6 Em
him for - ev - er. 8. Mountains and hills, bless the Lord. Bless the Lord, you
A7 D7 G6 Em G6 Em
grow - ing trees. 9. Springs of the earth, bless the Lord.
G6 Em A7 D7 G6 Em
Bless the Lord, you seas and riv - ers. 10. Crea-tures of the sea,
G6 Em G6 Em A7 D7
bless the Lord. Bless the Lord, you birds of the air.
G6 Em G6 Em G6 Em
11. Crea-tures wild and tame, bless the Lord. Praise and glo - ri - fy
A7 D7 G6 Em G6 Em
him for - ev - er. 12. Now let the Church bless the Lord.
G6 Em A7 D7 G6 Em
Let his peo-ple praise his name. 13. Priests of the Lord,

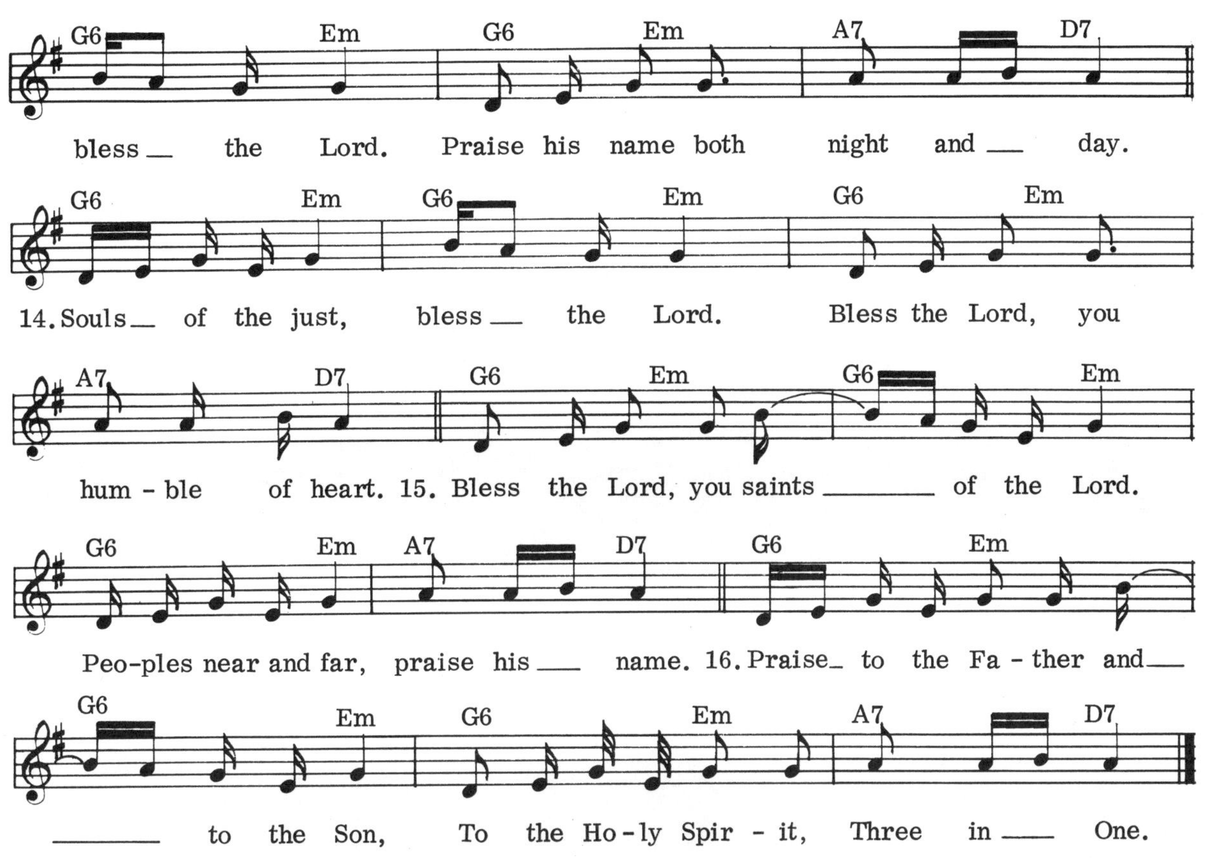

The Earth, O Lord, Belongs To Thee

Chester E. Custer | Lowell Mason, 1792-1872

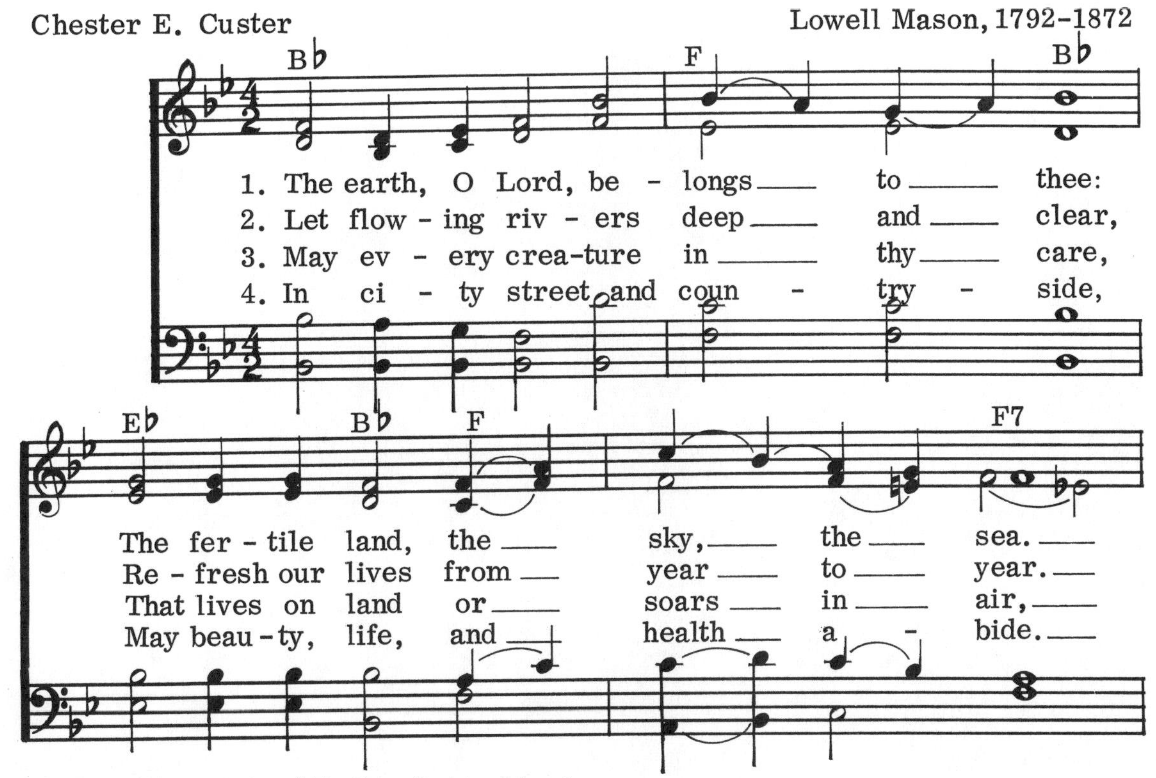

B♭ F B♭
O give us wis - dom in our age,
From streams de - filed we shall re - claim,
Be - hold the sun, the dis - tant shore,
Lo, all the waste - lands of our earth,
E♭ B♭ F B♭ E♭ B♭
To hold in trust our her - i - tage.
A cup of wa - ter in thy name.
And breathe the breath of life once more.
A - wait the day of sec - ond birth.
A - men.

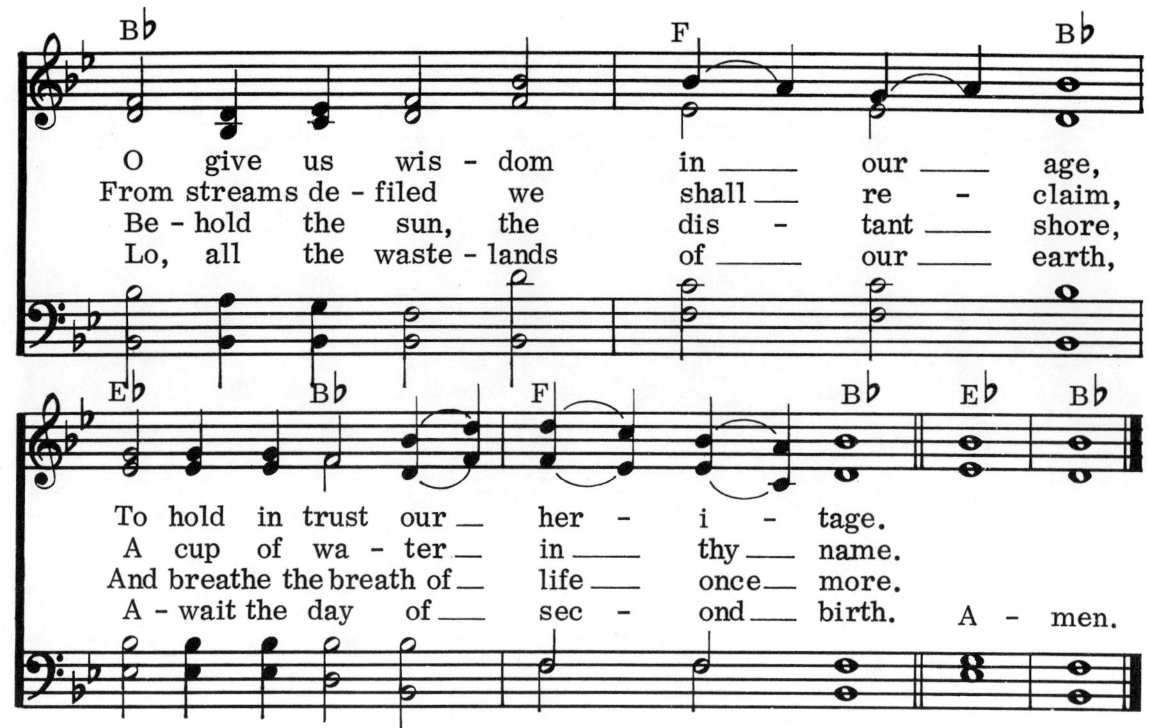

What Have They Done to the Rain?

Words and music by Malvina Reynolds

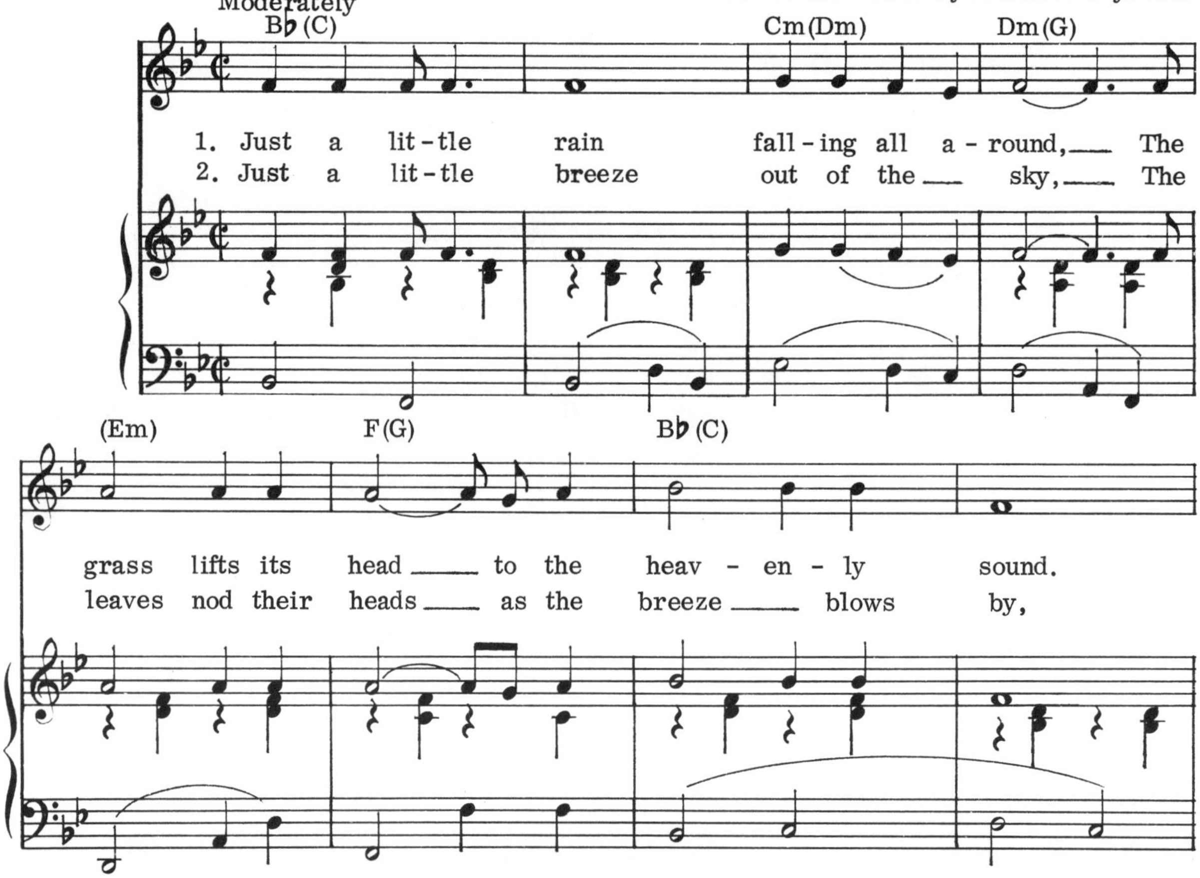

Moderately
B♭(C) Cm(Dm) Dm(G)
1. Just a lit - tle rain fall - ing all a - round, The
2. Just a lit - tle breeze out of the sky, The
(Em) F(G) B♭(C)
grass lifts its head to the heav - en - ly sound.
leaves nod their heads as the breeze blows by,

Gm(Am)
Dm(Em)
Just a lit - tle rain, just a lit - tle rain.
Just a lit - tle breeze with some smoke in its eye.
Eb(F)
F(G)
What have they done to the rain?
Bb(C)
Cm(Dm)
Dm(G)
Just a lit - tle boy stand-ing in the rain, The
(Em)
F7(G7)
Bb(C)
gen - tle rain that falls for years, And the

Gm(Am)
Dm(Em)
grass is gone, the boy dis - ap - pears, And
E♭(F)
B♭(C)
rain keeps fall - ing like help - less tears, And
Cm(Dm)
F(G)
first time
last time
what have they done to the rain?

Bread in the Wilderness

Very freely

Ewald Bash

1. Where shall we find bread__ in the wil - der - ness? they
2. Where shall we find bread__ for the mil - lions al - most
3. Who had loaves and fish - es for the hun - gry and their

said.__ O____ where shall we find bread or we die?
dead?__ O____ where shall we find bread for the earth?
wishes? O____ where shall we find bread or we die?

Mo - ses will you dare__ cry to God of our de -
Who can dare to speak__ of the u - ni - ty we
Mas - ter with thy bless-ing, break the loaves to us con -

spair?__ O____ how shall we be fed,__ for we
seek?__ O____ where shall we find bread__ and new
fess-ing, And to all____ the____ need-y world come

die?
birth? There is bread in the wil - der - ness and
by.

plen - ty to spare; Bread in the

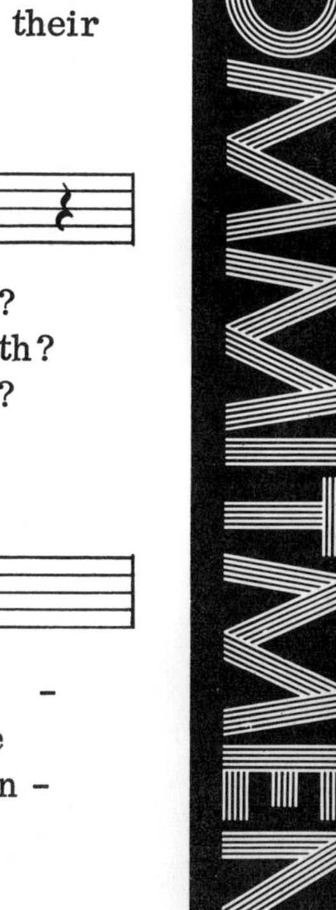

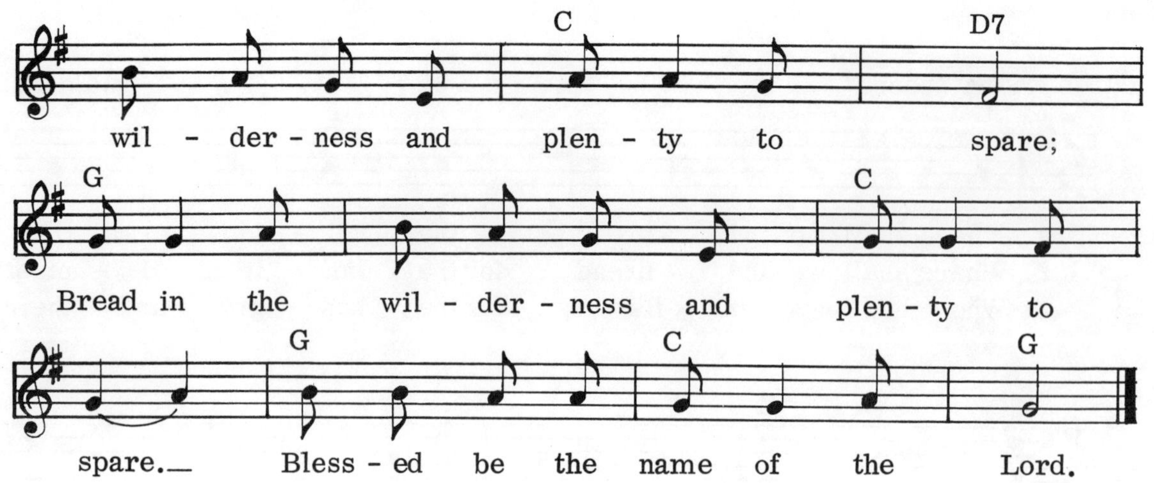

C D7
wil - der - ness and plen - ty to spare;
G C
Bread in the wil - der - ness and plen - ty to
G C G
spare.__ Bless - ed be the name of the Lord.

Feed Us Now

Peter Allen

Refrain
A D
Feed us now, O Son of God, As you
E7 A
fed them long a - go.
Verse
1. The
2. The
3. It's
4. Yet
5. So
A
peo - ple came to hear you,__ the poor, the lame, the
ones who did - n't lis - ten,__ the rich, the safe, the
hard for us to lis - ten,__ Things have - n't changed at
mill - ions still have hun - ger,__ Dis - ease, no homes, and
help us see the writ - ing, Writ - ten clear up - on the
A D
blind; They asked for food to
sure. They did - n't think they
all; We've got the things we
fear; We of - fer them so
wall: He who does - n't feed his

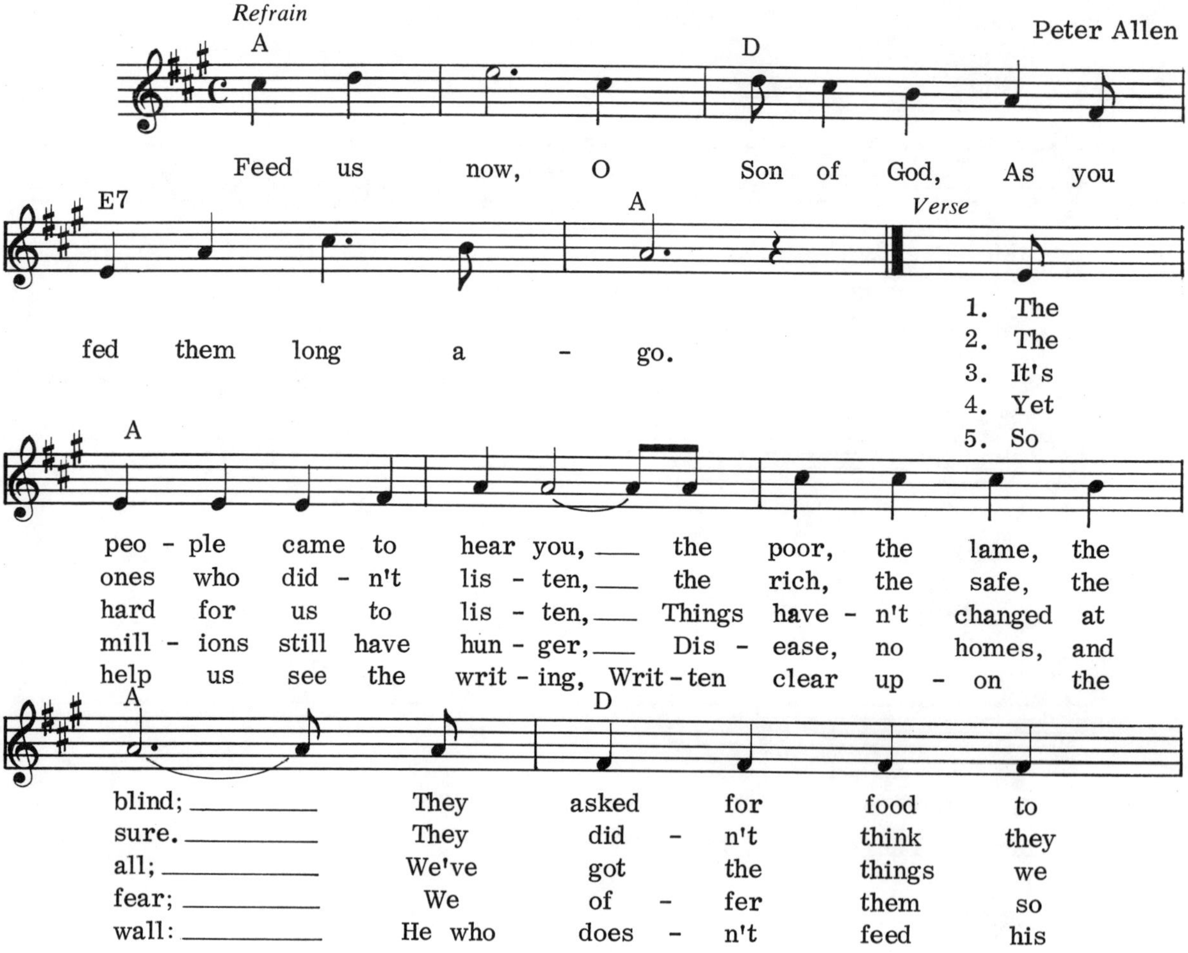

Bm
E7 to refrain
save them And you fed them, body and mind.
need - ed ___ The of - fering of a cure.
want - ed, We don't want to hear your call.
lit - tle, And it costs them ver - y dear.
neigh - bor ___ Will get no food at all.

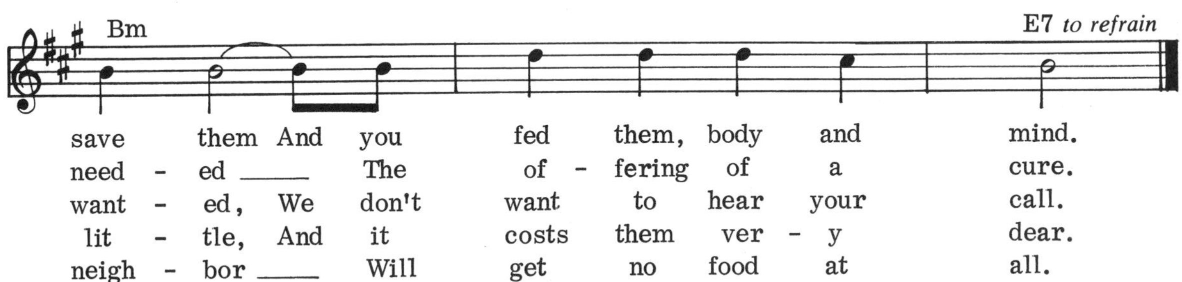

Have Mercy on the Wealthy

Marilyn Zakich
arr. by Bill Garrett

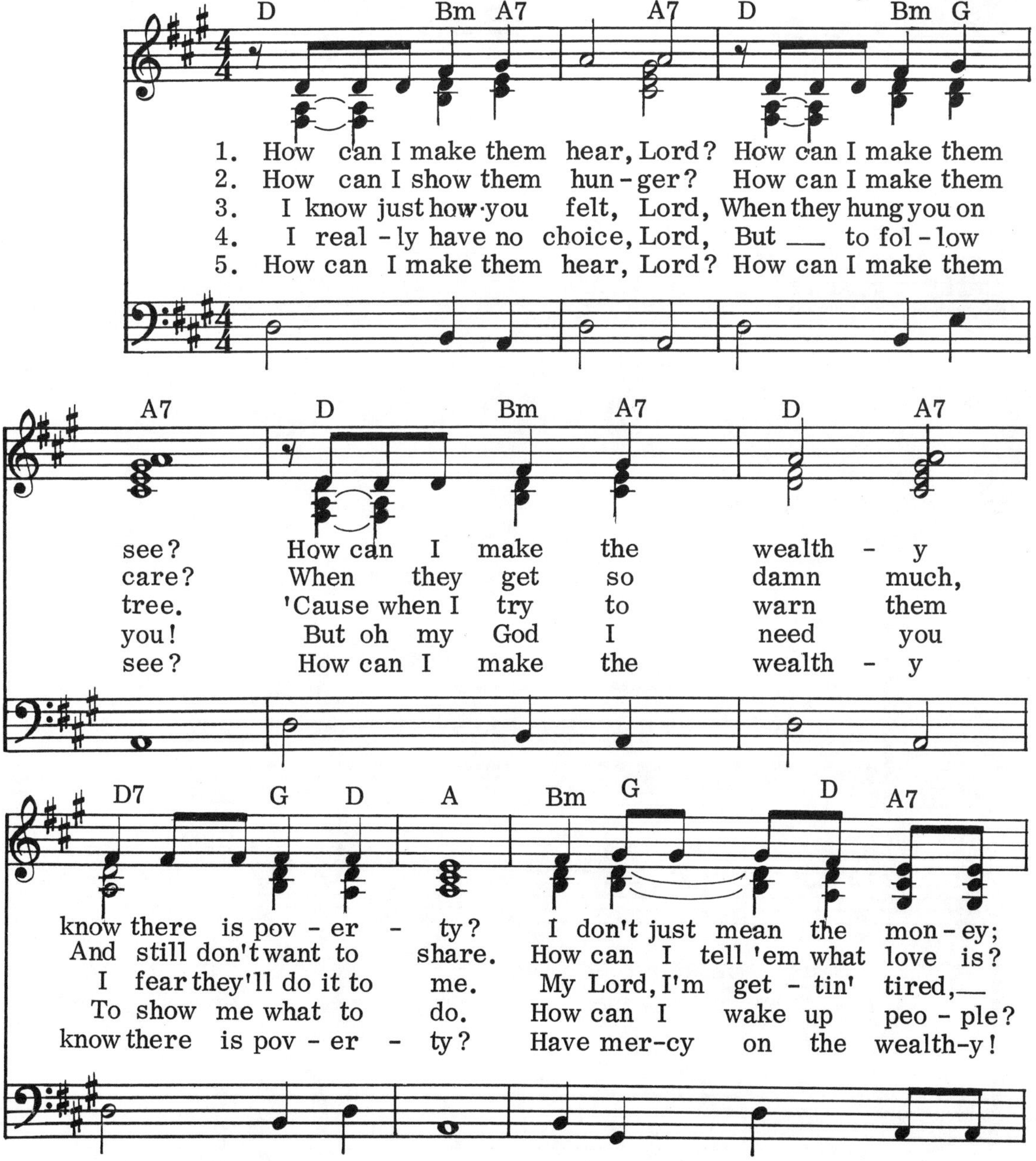

D Bm A7 A7 D Bm G
1. How can I make them hear, Lord? How can I make them
2. How can I show them hun - ger? How can I make them
3. I know just how you felt, Lord, When they hung you on
4. I real - ly have no choice, Lord, But ___ to fol - low
5. How can I make them hear, Lord? How can I make them
A7 D Bm A7 D A7
see? How can I make the wealth - y
care? When they get so damn much,
tree. 'Cause when I try to warn them
you! But oh my God I need you
see? How can I make the wealth - y
D7 G D A Bm G D A7
know there is pov - er - ty? I don't just mean the mon - ey;
And still don't want to share. How can I tell 'em what love is?
I fear they'll do it to me. My Lord, I'm get - tin' tired,—
To show me what to do. How can I wake up peo - ple?
know there is pov - er - ty? Have mer-cy on the wealth-y!

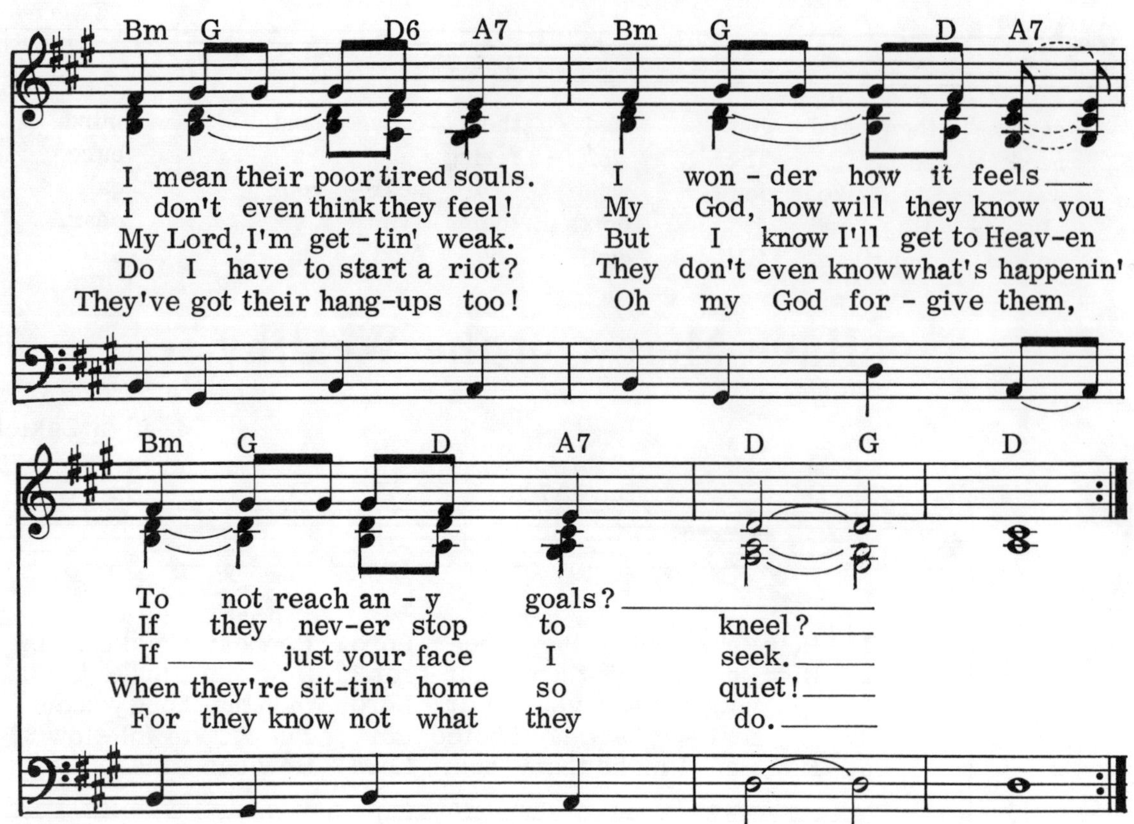

Let Us Break Bread Together

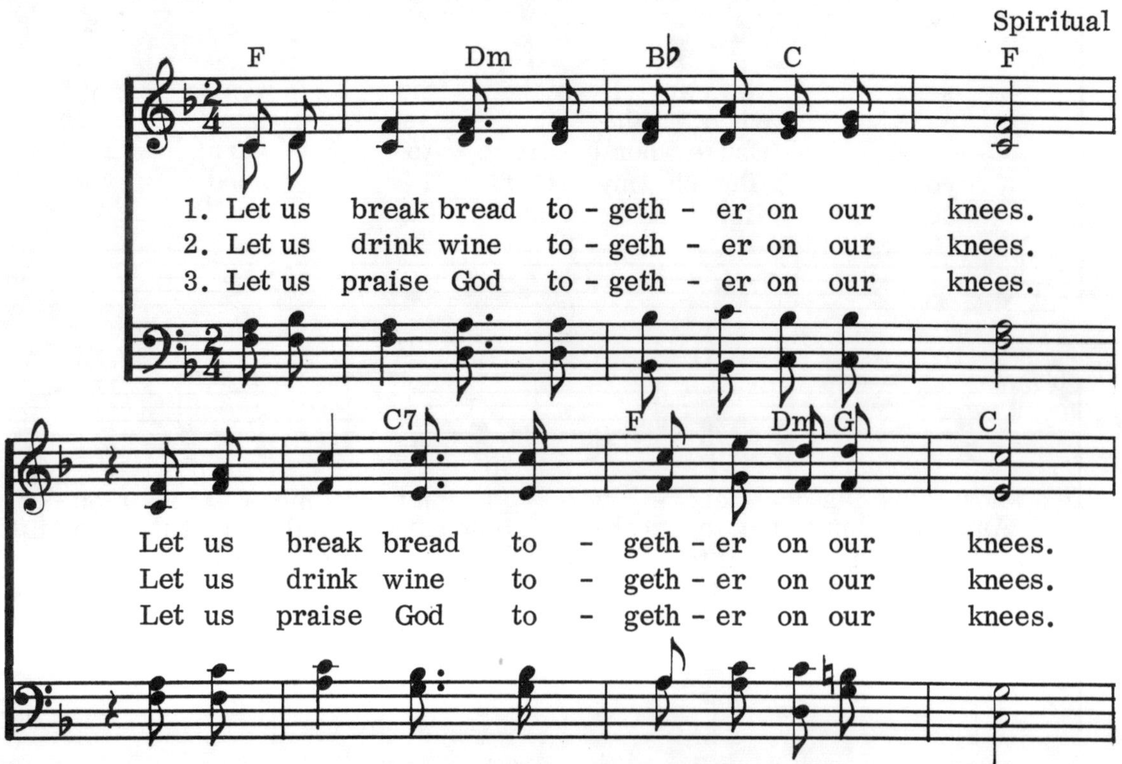

I Was Hungry

Words adapted, from Matthew 25:35-40

Arr. by Nick Hodsdon

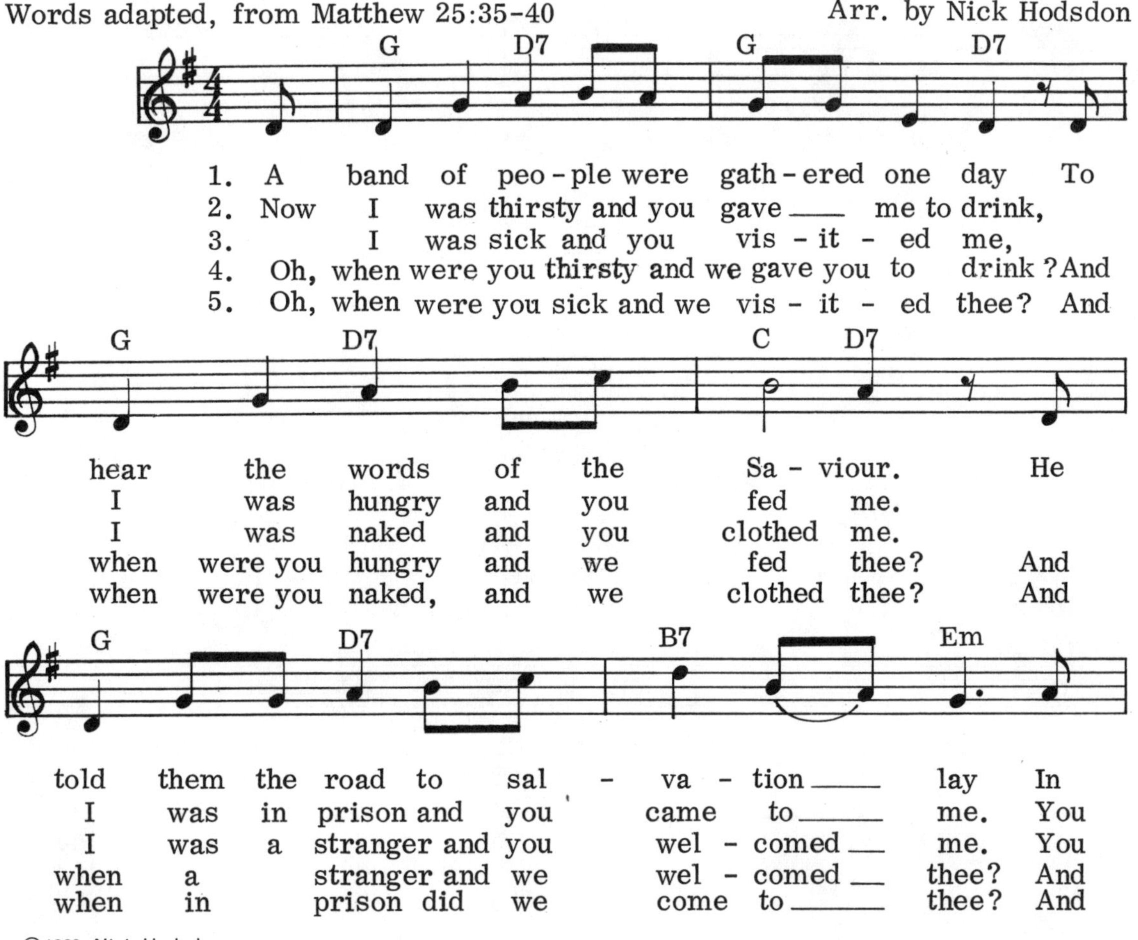

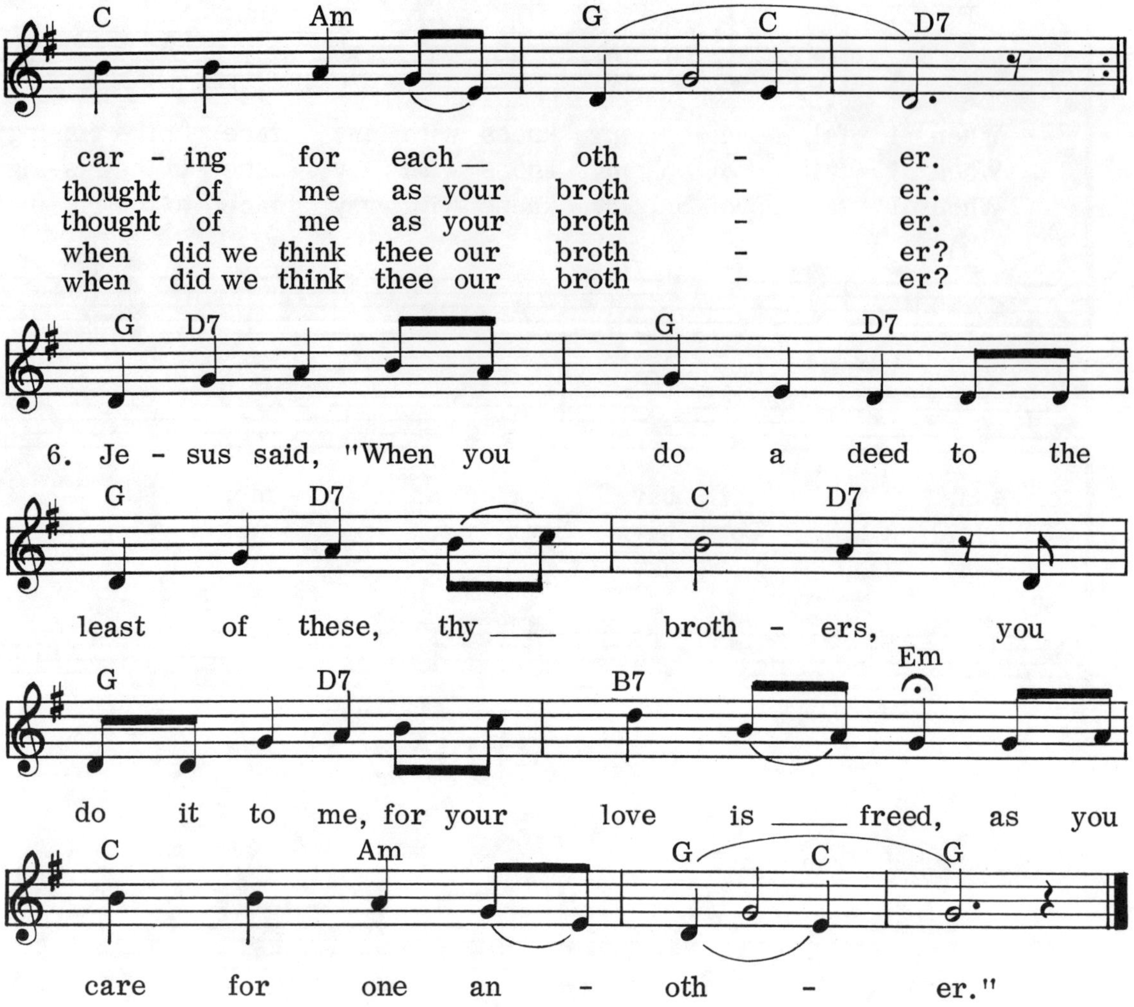

C Am G C D7
car - ing for each __ oth - er.
thought of me as your broth - er.
thought of me as your broth - er.
when did we think thee our broth - er?
when did we think thee our broth - er?
G D7 G D7
6. Je - sus said, "When you do a deed to the
G D7 C D7
least of these, thy ___ broth - ers, you
G D7 B7 Em
do it to me, for your love is ____ freed, as you
C Am G C G
care for one an - oth - er."

Sixteen Chapel

R. K. Hudnut J. L. Bell

Fm Db
1. We went to the Six - teen
2. They told me to mind ___ my
3. I told them that may - be
4. Was Je - sus, I thought,_ called
5. They stayed in the Six - teen
6. Now I am in jail ____ in
Fm Fm Db
Chap - el. ____ I went to a bar down the
busi - ness. ___ We must, they ex - plained, go whole
peo - ple ____ In church-es should lurch to the
ho - ly, ____ Be - cause he went in to the
Chap - el. ____ I went from the bar to the
Rom - a. ____ The chap - el still stands with its

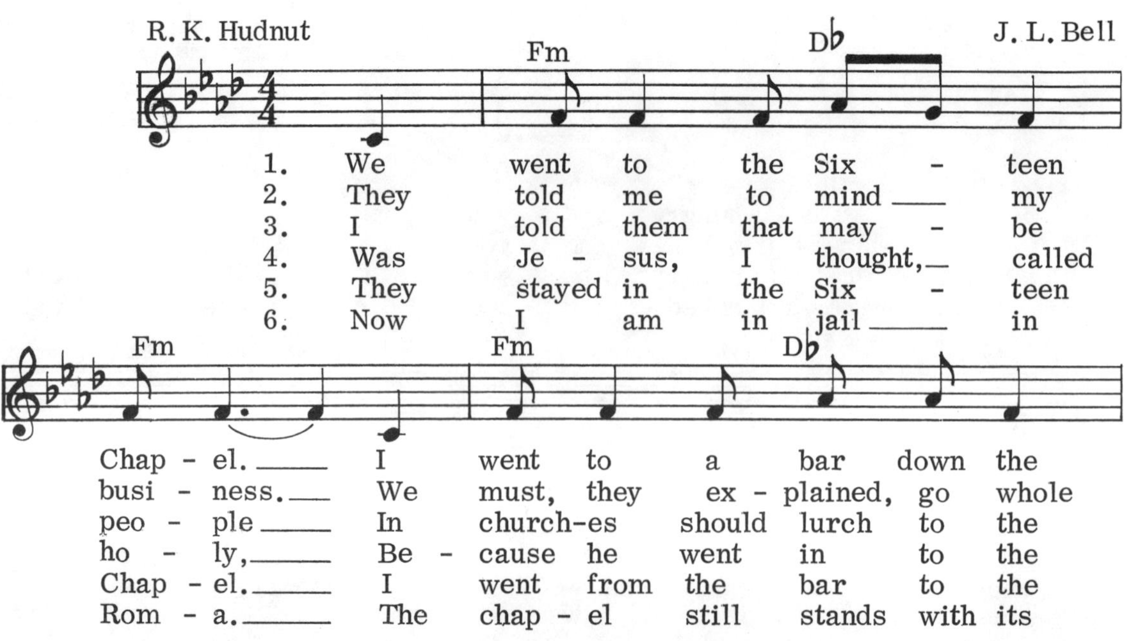

Fm
Db
Fm
street. All them dia - monds, all that gold, The
hog. Other-wise no one will lurch From
bars, Be - cause there they could find out What
church? Or was it be - cause he went To
street. There I met an or - phan child So
art. But the child is dressed and fed, And
Db
C
Bbm
art that was so old. I told them if that was re -
bars to come to church, And peo - ple in bars need sal -
peo - ple think a - bout, And church peo - ple need ed - u -
church in bars and spent His time with the lost and the
hun - gry and so wild. I gave her the gold from the
mil - lions now have bread. It may be that this is re -
C
1.
Fm
Fm
li - gion ...
va - tion.
ca - tion.
lone - ly?
tem - ple.
li - gion.
2.
Fm
Fm
Fm

Here We Are

Refrain
Ray Repp
Here we are all to-geth-er as we sing our song joy-ful-ly. Here we are joined to-geth-er as we pray we'll al-ways be.
Verses
1. Join we now as friends, and cel-e-brate the
5. Let us make the world an Al-le-lu-ia!
1. Broth-er-hood we share all as one.
5. Let us make the world a bet-ter place.
1. Keep the fire burn-ing, kin-dle it with care,
5. Keep a smile hand-y, have a help-ing hand,
1. And we'll all join in and sing.
5. Let us all join in and sing.
2. Free-dom we do shout for ev-'ry-bod-y,
2. And, un-less there is, we should pray that

C Am F G7
2. soon there will be one true broth - er - hood;—

C Am F G7
2. Let us all join — in and sing. —

C Am F G7
3. Glo - ri - fy the Lord with all our voic - es
4. Hap - py is the man who does his best to

C Am F G7
3. Show him we're sin - cere by all our deeds.
4. Free the trou-bled world from all its pain.

C Am F G7
3. Shout the joys of free - dom ev - 'ry - where,—
4. Join we with that man and free the world,—

C Am F G7
3. And we'll all join — in and sing. —
4. As we all join — in and sing. —

When All Men Shall Walk Together

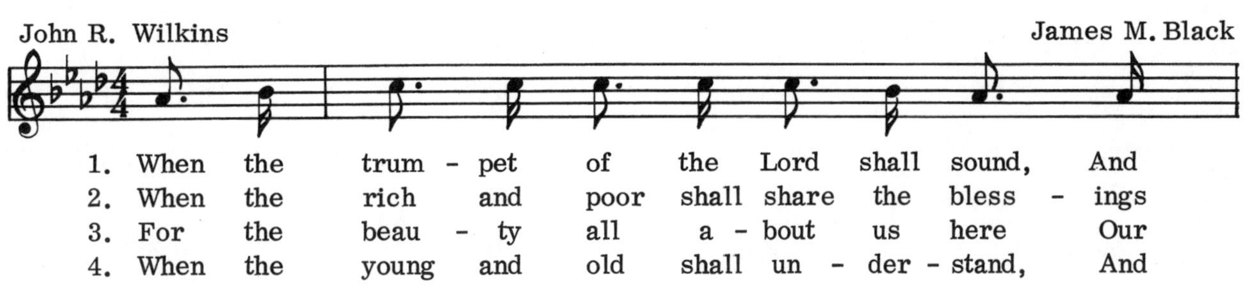

Words used by permission of John R. Wilkins

guns shall be no more, When the paths of peace are o - pen far and
of this world of ours, And the Lord shall wipe a - way our hates and
minds are full of thanks; For pure wa - ter and clear air we breathe a
dreams shall come to life; And the call of God shall ring in ev - ery
wide, And when men shall cease their fight - ing And shall
fears; When the black and brown and white shall walk As
prayer; When we use them and we save them For the
mind, And we live with faith and cour - age Je - sus
build a broth - er - hood. Then the
friends up - on this earth, Then the
chil - dren yet to come, Then this
showed up - on the cross; Then the
love of Christ shall rule in ev - ery
love of Christ shall rule in ev - ery
earth shall be a joy for - ev - er -
king - dom of our Lord shall come to
Refrain
heart.
heart.
more.
pass
When all men shall walk to - geth - er, when all
men shall walk to - geth - er, When all
men shall walk to - geth - er, Then the
love of Christ shall rule in ev - ery heart.

Sons of God

KEY: F CAPO: 1st PLAY: E

James Thiem

Refrain

F(E) Dm(C♯m) B♭(A) C7(B7)
Sons of God, hear His holy Word!
F(E) Dm(C♯m) B♭(A) C7(B7)
Gather 'round the table of the Lord!
F(E) Dm(C♯m) B♭(A) C7(B7)
Eat His Body, drink His Blood.
F(E) Dm(C♯m) B♭(A) C7(B7)
And we'll sing a song of love: Alle-
F(E) Dm(C♯m) B♭(A) C7(B7)
lu, al-le-lu, al-le-lu, al-le-lu-

1-6. F(E) Dm(C♯m) B♭(A) C7(B7)
ia!

7. F(E) B♭(A) F(E)
ia!

F(E) Dm(C♯m) B♭(A) C7(B7)
1. Brothers, sisters, we are one,
2. Shout together to the Lord
3. Jesus gave a new command
4. If we want to live with Him,
5. Make the world a unity,
6. With the church we celebrate,

F(E) Dm(C♯m) B♭(A) C7(B7)
And our life has just begun;
Who has promised our reward:
That we love our fellow man
We must also die with Him,
Make all men one family
Jesus' coming we await;

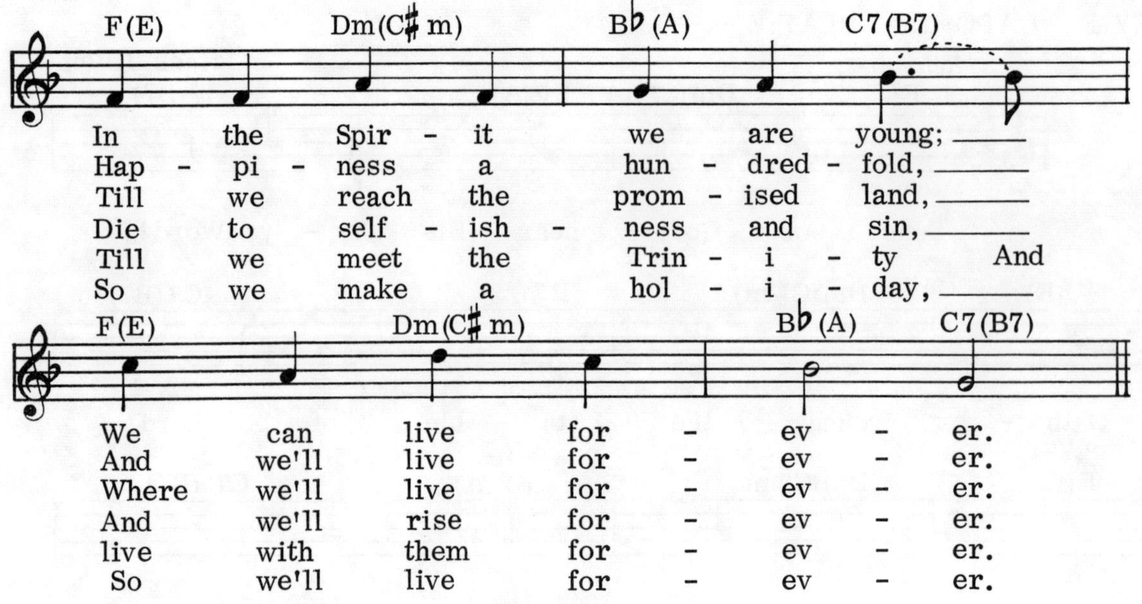

Take Our Bread

Moderately

Joe Wise

C *Refrain* Am

Take our bread, we ask you; take our

F Dm C

hearts, we love you. Take our lives, oh

Dm G7 C

Fa - ther, we are yours, we are yours.

Verses C Am C

1. Yours as we stand at the ta - ble you

Am C F Dm

set; Yours as we eat the bread our hearts can't for -

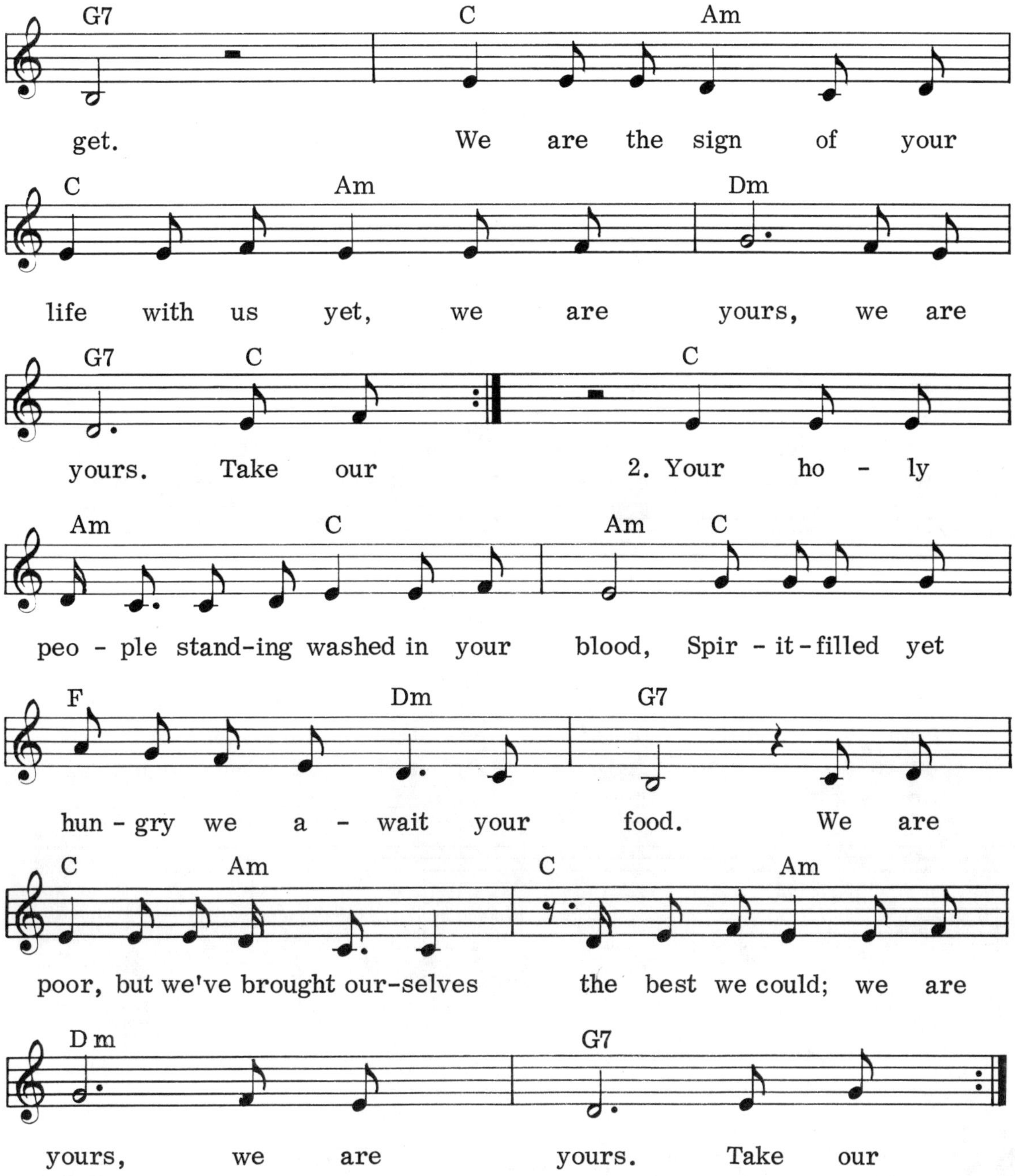

G7 C Am
get. We are the sign of your
C Am Dm
life with us yet, we are yours, we are
G7 C C
yours. Take our 2. Your ho - ly
Am C Am C
peo - ple stand-ing washed in your blood, Spir - it - filled yet
F Dm G7
hun - gry we a - wait your food. We are
C Am C Am
poor, but we've brought our-selves the best we could; we are
Dm G7
yours, we are yours. Take our

They'll Know We are Christians By Our Love

Words and Music by Peter Scholtes

Fm
1. We are one in the Spir - it, we are
2. We will walk with each oth - er, we will
3. We will work with each oth - er, we will
4. All ___ praise to the Fath - er, From ___

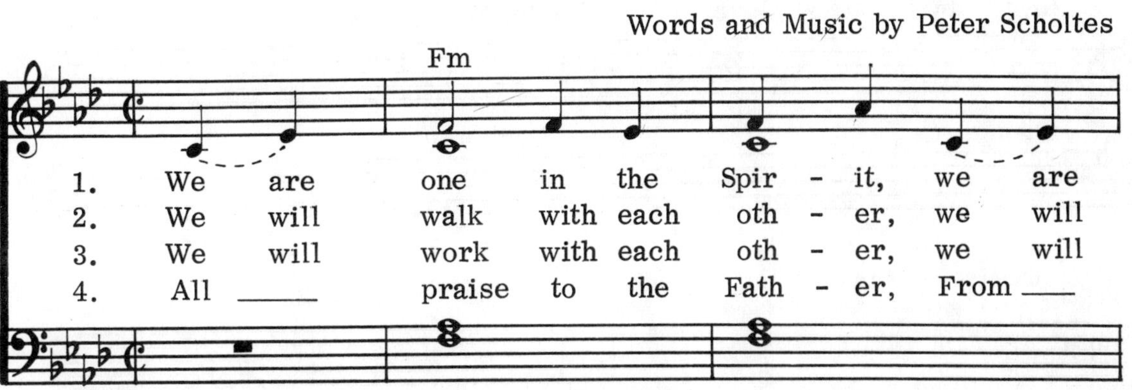

B♭m
one in the Lord, We are one in the
walk hand in hand, We will walk with each
work side by side, We will work with each
whom all things come, And all praise to Christ
Fm
Spir - it, we are one in the Lord, And we
oth - er, we will walk hand in hand, And to -
oth - er, we will work side by side, And we'll
Je - sus, His on - ly Son, And all
B♭m
Fm
pray that all u - ni - ty may one day be re -
geth - er we'll spread the news that God is in our
guard each man's dig - ni - ty and save each man's
praise to the Spir - it, who makes us
Refrain:
D♭
stored,
land,
pride,
one,
And they'll know we are Christ-ians by our
Fm
B♭
Fm
love, by our love, Yes, they'll know we are
B♭m
E♭
Fm
Christ - ians by our love.

appendix a

"CELEBRATION"

(a contemporary Communion Service)

INTRODUCTION

Through the years, man has sought to worship God in the symbolism and art forms that he best understands. While he believes we worship an Eternal Being, we are nevertheless finite and products of our own culture. What may have therefore been meaningful expressions in past generations may be quite outdated today.

The celebration of Holy Communion has remained somewhat the same through the years because essentially the Church has believed that this is the point where God and man interact in fellowship and reconciliation.

As we trace the history of language and music, we discover that the words to the ritual (although undergoing transition from Greek to Latin to English) are essentially the same, or at least similar.

The music written for the service, however, has evolved from chant to plainsong and hymnody, and now often is expressed as folk type music adaptable to guitar accompaniment.

The following service has been called "The Celebration," for that is exactly what it is. We "celebrate" the fact that God through Christ has delivered us from death to life. Too often Holy Communion has been something mournful. But it is time that we as Christians learn to "celebrate." The dictionary defines celebration as "proclamation, honoring, commemorating and observing a significant event." We do this in remembrance of Christ, as he has commanded us, and thus he has promised to be present at the table with us.

This particular setting of the service is adaptable for use in the church sanctuary, around the tables in the fellowship hall, at the lakeside, or around the campfire. The liturgist should train singers in advance, to help carry the congregation in their part of the service.

The various parts of the service explain themselves. The mood seems to alternate between the praise of God and the recognition of man's condition. We are on the one hand sorry for what we are, but on the other hand thankful for who He is. It is a celebration for man the "lost child who has come home again"; the dead son who has come back to life. (Luke 15:24)

Norman K. Silvester, 1968

NOTE: There may be occasions when it is not feasible to observe communion. In that event, any of the hymns and responses may be adapted to a folksong service as seems appropriate.

All Praise Be to our God and King

(Congregational hymn or Call to Worship, as preferred)

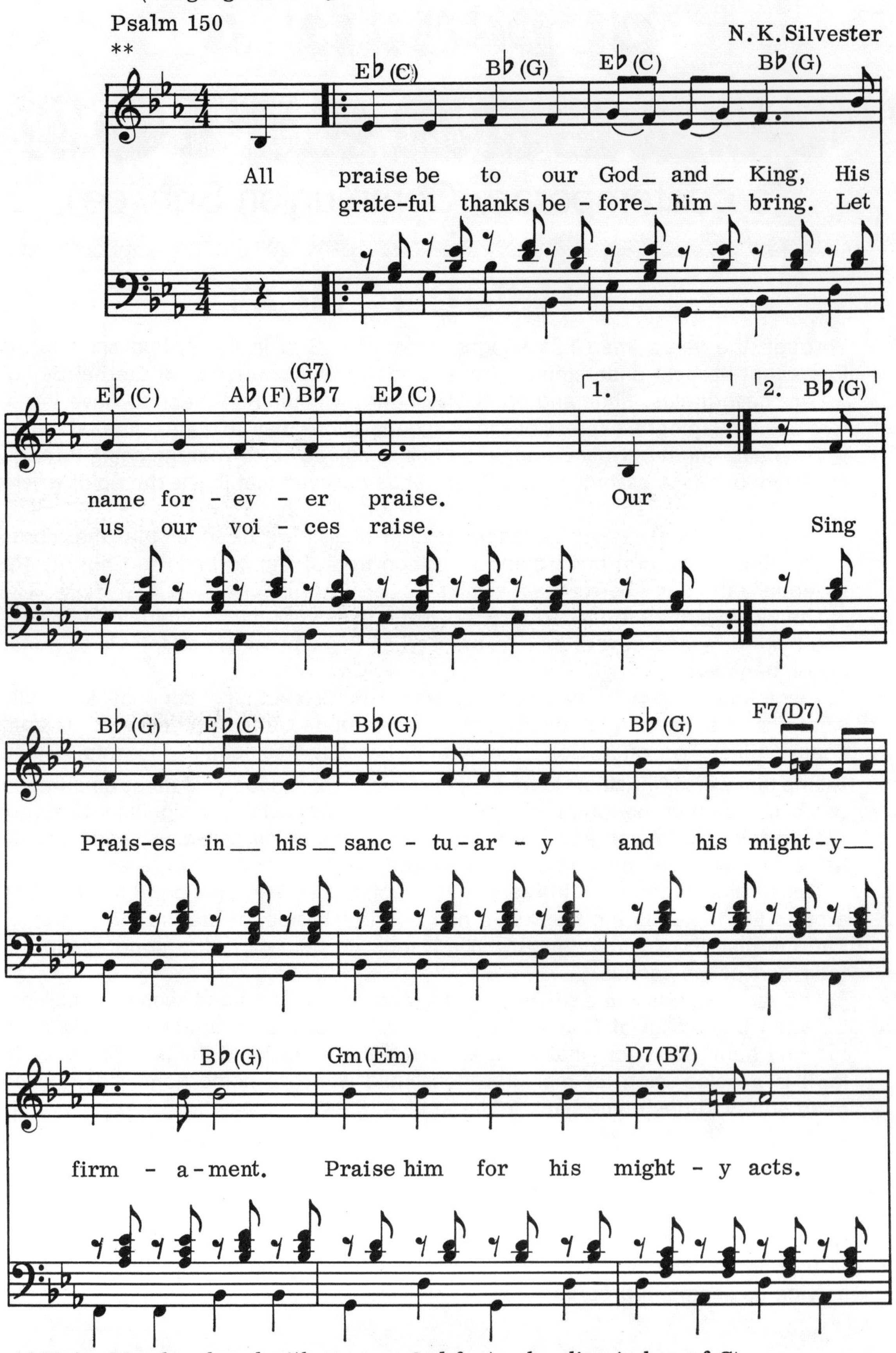

**(Note: May be played with capo on 3rd fret, chording in key of C)

Gm(Em) Eb(C) Bb7(G7)
Praise him for — his great - ness. Praise him for — his —
Eb(C) Bb7(G7) Eb(C) Bb7(G7)
pow - er. Praise him for — his — glo - ry.
Eb(C) Bb7 (G7) Eb(C) Bb7(G7) Eb(C) Bb7(G7)
All that now has life — and — breath, sing prais-es to the
(Hold 2nd time only.)
Eb(C)
Fine
Ab(F) Eb(C)
Lord. Praise him with trumpet sound. Praise him with
Bb7(G7) Eb(C) Ab(F) Eb(C)
lute and harp. Praise him with dan - cing song.

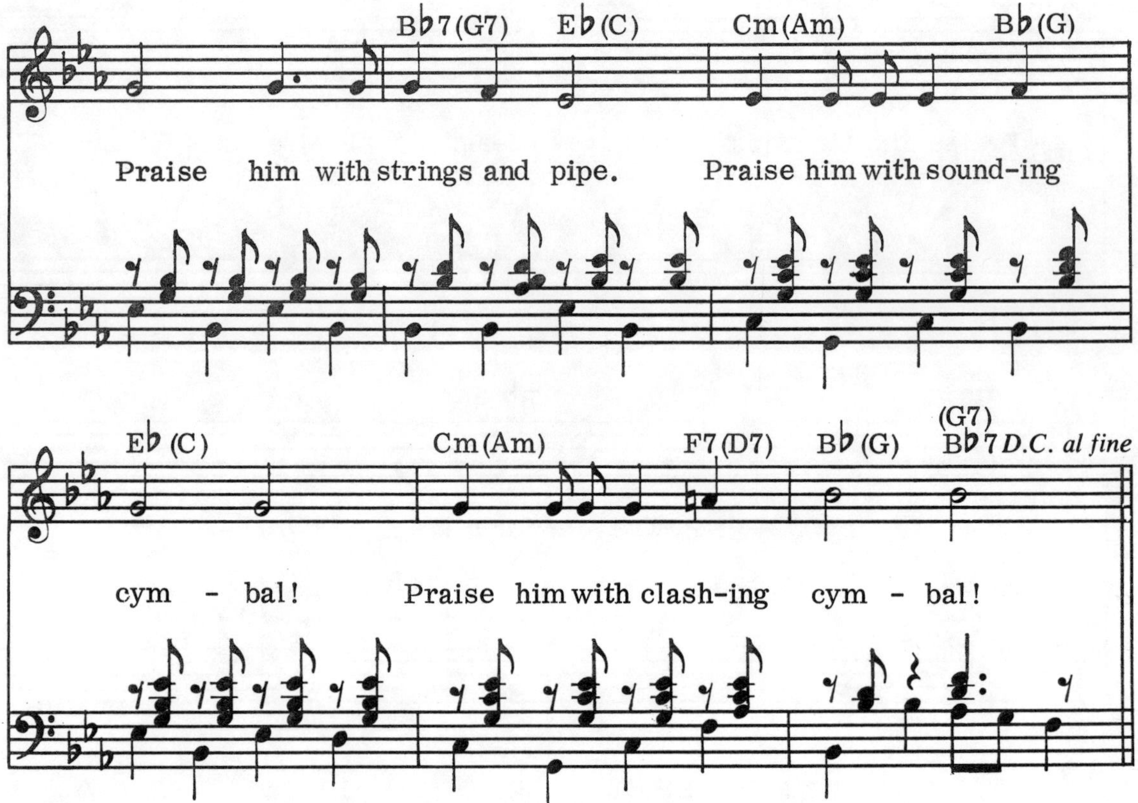

Prayer of Confession: (All uniting)

Mighty and merciful Father, we have turned aside from Your ways like lost sheep. We have looked for the things *we* want instead of what *You* want. We have *not* done what we *should* have, and *have* done what we should *not* have. But Lord, have mercy. We confess our mistakes. Bring us back as You have promised You would, through Jesus Christ our Lord. Grant that from now on we may live, for Him, a godly and straight life, to the glory of Your holy name. Amen.

Response: "Have Mercy upon Us, Lord" (Kyrie)

Have Mercy upon Us, Lord

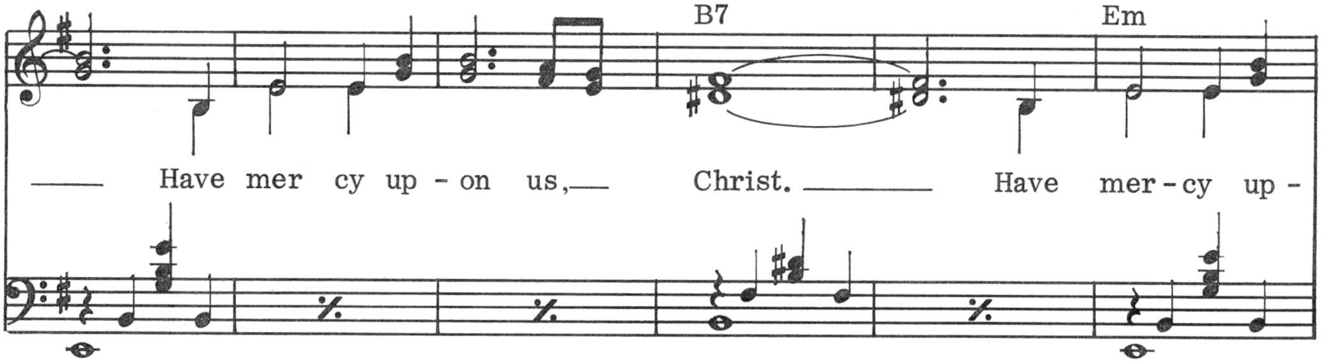

B7
Em
Have mer cy up - on us, Christ. Have mer-cy up -

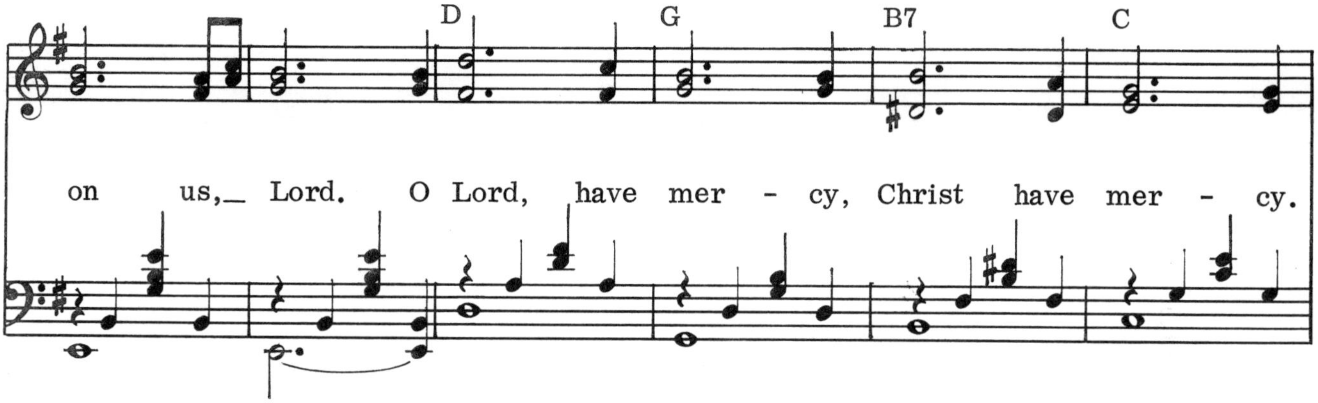

D
G
B7
C
on us, Lord. O Lord, have mer - cy, Christ have mer - cy.

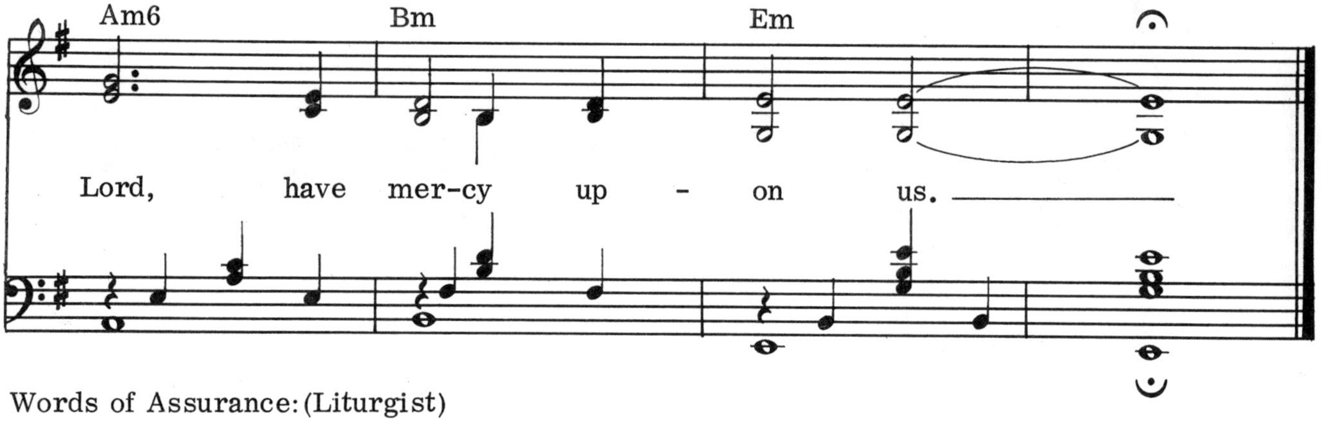

Am6
Bm
Em
Lord, have mer-cy up - on us.

Words of Assurance: (Liturgist)

All Glory Be to God on High

(Gloria in Excelsis Deo)
(alternate tune)

N. K. Silvester

C
G7
C
G7
C
A
(Introduction)
1. All glo - ry be to
2. Al - might - y Fa - ther,
3. O Lord, now seat - ed at
(guitar or string bass countermelody)

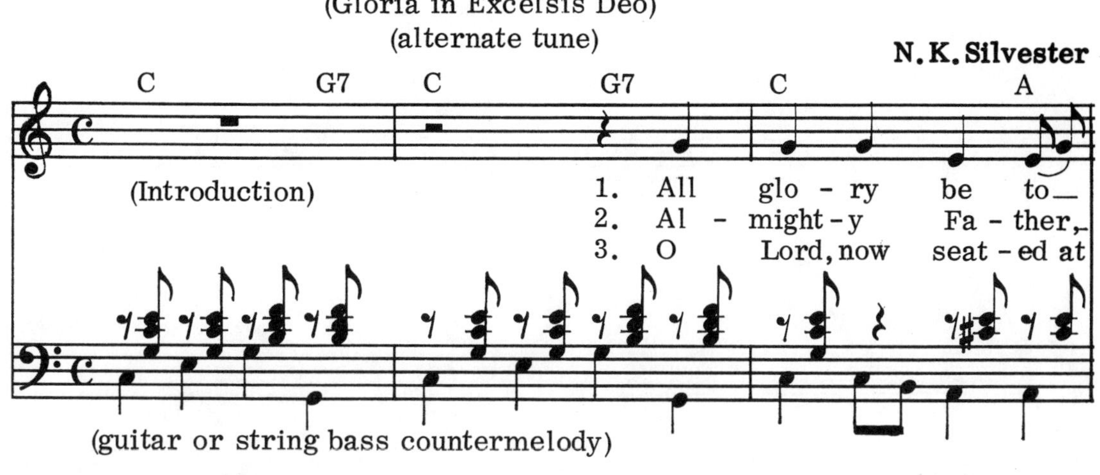

(Note: Here may follow the Scripture, Creed, and Sermon.)

O My God, You Have Known Me

May the Lord Be with You

(Sursum Corda and Sanctus)

C Am D Am
You, O Lord, ho - ly Fa - ther, Al - might - y ev - er - last - ing
D C D
God. There-fore with an - gels and all arch-
C D Am D
an - gels and all the com-pa-ny of Heav'n we
C D Am D Am
laud and mag - ni - fy your ho - ly name,
D Am D C D C
ev - er -more prais - ing You and say - ing:
All Uniting:
D C D C D C D C D C
Ho - ly, Ho-ly, Ho - ly, Lord, God of Hosts: Heav'n and earth are

NOTE: (Then shall follow the consecration of the Bread and the Cup)

Prayer of Humble Access: (All Uniting)

We do not expect to come to Your Table, merciful Lord, because we are righteous, but because You are merciful to us. We do not even deserve the leftovers, but we come believing that by Your grace You have invited us. And so we want to partake of this Holy Celebration in a way that will make us walk in Christ's love, that we might grow in his likeness, and live in his fellowship forever. Amen.

Response: "O Lamb of God" (Agnus Dei)

have mercy on us
O Lamb of God
(Agnus Dei)
N. K. Silvester
C Em F G7 C Em
O Lamb of God, who
F G7 C Am Dm G7
takes a - way the sins of the world, have mer - cy on us.
C Em F G7 C Am
O Lamb of God, who takes a-way the sins of the world, have

(Partaking of the Holy Sacrament)

O Bless the Lord, My Soul

Psalm 103

N. K. Silvester

Dm F C D C F
soul. O bless the Lord, my soul.
ful. For he is mer - ci - ful.
sin. He par - dons all your sin.
bove. High as the heav'n a - bove.
shows. Fa-ther-ly love he shows.
grass. Frail as the bloom - ing flow'r.
throne. He has es-tab - lished his throne.
Dm C F Gm Dm C
And all with - in sing praise un - to Him.
And he is pa - tient, gra - cious and kind.
Re - deems your life from sick - ness and death.
So great to us his un - chang-ing love.
He pit - ies us and knows all our ways.
From ev - er - last - ing His love shall stand.
Though king-doms fall, he rules o - ver all.
O bless the Lord, my
Dm Dm C D
(After last verse only)
soul. O bless the Lord, my soul.

appendix b

GUITAR CHORDS

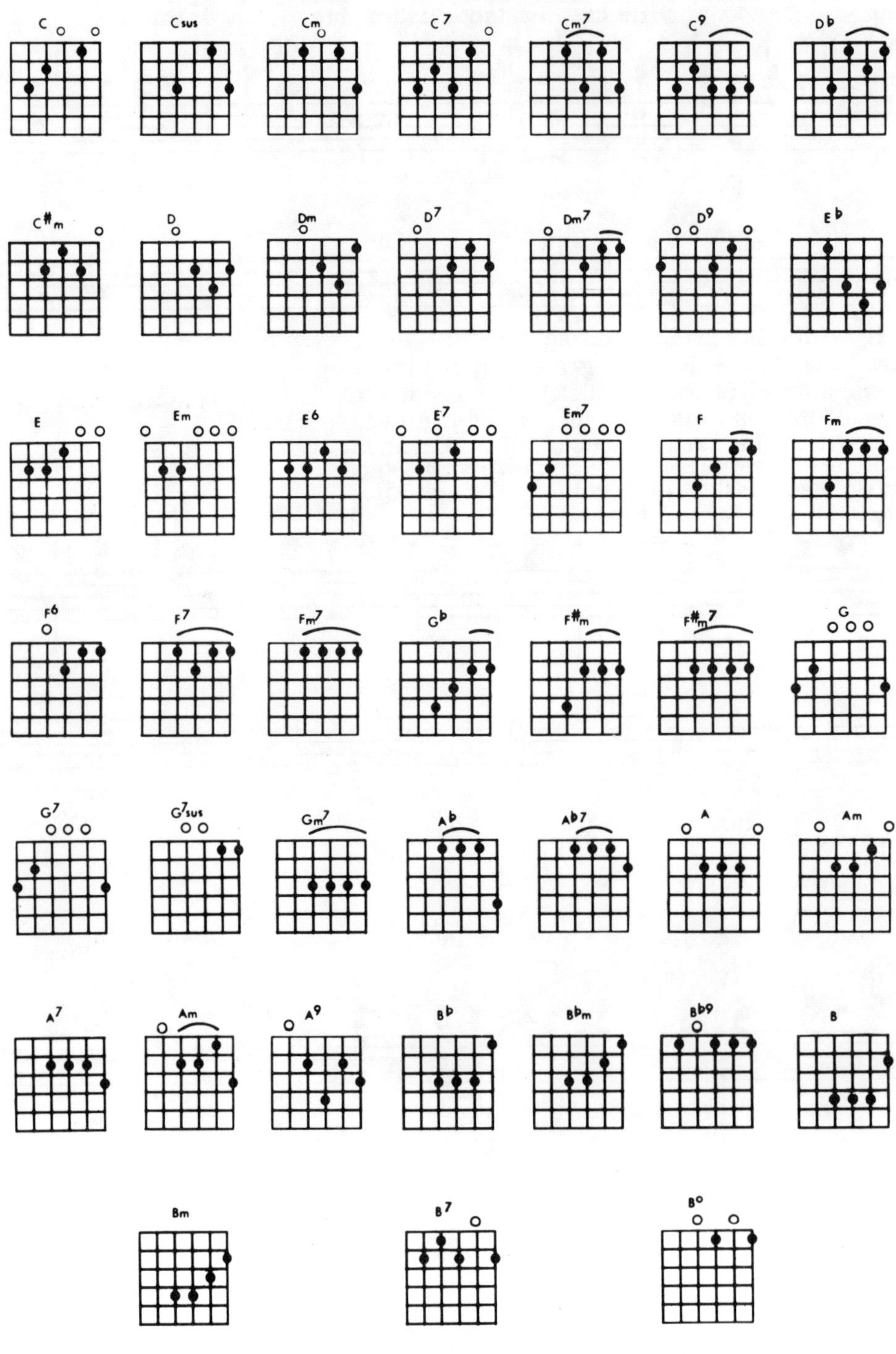

Index of Songs

TURESINSONG
EDITED BY
RANDOLPH
for the
WORSHIP of THE UNITED
HODIST CHURCH
SISTANCE FROM BILL GARRETT
NGDON PRESS
NEW YORK
the end
VENTURESIN

G-bye!
VENTURES IN SONG

EDITED BY

DAVID J. RANDOLPH

WITH SPECIAL ASSISTANCE FROM BILL GARRETT

"'Ventures in Song' is a collection of songs for a pilgrimage. The collection is a contribution to a global search—a search for new meaning and a search for more adequate ways to express meaning."

—from the Foreword

This exciting songbook marks a positive move toward updating the music of today's church. It is a versatile collection which may be used as a songbook, a supplement to the church's existing hymnal, or as a complement to the popular worship series "Ventures in Worship" and "Ventures in Worship 2," edited by David J. Randolph and published by Abingdon.

The songs themselves encompass a wide range of musical types, including traditional spirituals which have significance for today, familiar hymn tunes with modern lyrics, and all new songs written by today's youthful poets and prophets. Most of the selections include guitar chords and full piano accompaniment.

Because today's churches are experiencing a reawakening and many are renewing the celebrative designs in their worship services, "Ventures in Song" may be only the beginning.

DAVID J. RANDOLPH is assistant general secretary of the General Board of Evangelism of The United Methodist Church, Christian Community Section. Author, editor, and former pastor, Dr. Randolph preaches and lectures widely. His work also involves planning New Life Missions, which seek to renew and mobilize the local church for mission, and Leisure Ministries, which reach into resorts and urban entertainment areas.

Bill Garrett is pastor of Venice Park United Methodist Church, Atlantic City, New Jersey.

255-195 AN ABINGDON ORIGINAL PAPERBACK